THE WILD WEST
MEETS THE BIG APPLE

THE WILD WEST
MEETS THE BIG APPLE

MICHAEL P. O'CONNOR

PELICAN PUBLISHING COMPANY

GRETNA 2016

ISBN: 9781455621682
E-book ISBN: 9781455621699

Printed in Malaysia
Published by Pelican Publishing Company, Inc.
1000 Burmaster Street, Gretna, Louisiana 70053

*This book is dedicated to the memory
of Sgt. John F. O'Connor (NYPD) (1930–2012)—
A cowboy at heart*

CONTENTS

ACKNOWLEDGMENTS

I started writing this book because the subject interested me. I was really writing for myself. As the manuscript evolved, I began to realize that if I wanted anyone, besides me, to be able to read the finished project, I needed a whole lot of help. Fortunately, I received that help.

When it became apparent that I did not have the technological capability to transform my work from Pages into printer-ready pages with page numbers, chapters, and photo images, I scoured the internet for some guidance. Luckily I came across the webpage of Stephen Tiano, Book Designer, Page Compositor & Layout Artist. Not only did Stephen design and format the book; he designed the cover and was a constant source of guidance in assisting me through this somewhat baffling process of getting a book published. I couldn't have done it without you, Stephen.

As fate would have it, the son-in-law of my best friend, Christopher Rosenbluth, just happens to be a Professor of English Professor at New Mexico State University. He graciously agreed to edit the manuscript. He did a superb job. I'm embarrassed (but grateful) to admit that he corrected thousands of errors. Thanks, Chris.

I would also like to thank Elliot Linzer who went above and beyond in creating the index, and Nina Kooij, along with the entire staff at Pelican Publishing for their patience with a first-time author. Thanks, guys.

Last, but certainly not least, I would like to thank my family—my loving wife of over 30 years, Laura; my sons, Patrick and Sean; my daughter Margie; and my son-in-law, Kevin Cuomo. In addition to giving me the time I needed, they all contributed in some way to the completion of this book (pictures, research, advice, and encouragement). It did not go unnoticed or unappreciated. Love you all.

New York City Timeline
During the Settling
of the West

1812   New York's City Hall opens. The United
States and England clash in the War of 1812.

1817   Formation of New York Stock and
Exchange Board.
David Crockett becomes a justice of the
peace in Lawrence County, Tennessee.

1823   Niblo's Gardens begins operating as an
outside venue serving coffee and lemonade.
David Crockett is reelected to the
Tennessee State Legislature.

1824   Castle Clinton reopens on July 3 as Castle
Gardens.

1825   The first opera performed in the United
States, Rossini's *Barber of Seville*, opens at
the Park Theater.
The Erie Canal is opened.
The American Hotel opens.

1826   The Bowery Theater opens.
1827   Slavery is abolished in New York.
        Delmonico's Restaurant starts operations in
        New York City.
        David Crockett is elected to Congress.
        James Bowie is severely injured but emerges a
        legend in the Sandbar Fight.
1833   James Bowie and his brother Rezin visit New
        York City.
1834   April–May, Col. David Crockett visits New York
        City.
        Construction of the Astor House on Broadway
        begins.
1835   Devastating fire destroys over 700 buildings in
        downtown New York City.
        On November 30, Samuel Clemens is born in
        Florida, Missouri.
        David Crockett is defeated in what would be his
        last bid for Congress.
1836   On March 6, Col. David Crockett is among the
        fallen heroes of the battle of the Alamo in San
        Antonio, Texas.
        The prestigious Union Club is formed in New
        York City.
        Crockett nemesis and New Yorker Martin Van
        Buren is elected president.
1837   On May 27, Wild Bill Hickok is born in Troy
        Grove, Illinois.
        In July, West Point cadet William Sherman
        attends his theatrical performance at the Park
        Theater.

1841   First issue of Horace Greeley's *New York Tribune* is published.

Congress appropriates $30,000 to pay for a survey of the Oregon Trail and names Lt. John C. Fremont to head the expedition.

1846   The United States declares war on Mexico.

John C. Fremont declares California part of the United States.

On February 26, Buffalo Bill Cody is born in LeClaire, Iowa.

1848   Project begins to extend the Battery to incorporate Castle Gardens into the park.

Park Theater burns down and never reopens.

On March 29, fur mogul John Jacob Astor dies in New York City at the age of 84.

1849   Astor Place riot leaves over 20 New Yorkers dead. Ned Buntline would ultimately serve a year in jail for being one of the instigators.

Gold Prospectors rush to California.

1853   On July 14, President Franklin Pierce opens the World's Fair at the Crystal Palace at what is now Bryant Park. A young Samuel Clemens is among the visitors.

The St. Nicholas Hotel opens.

On November 26, Bat Masterson is born in Quebec, Canada.

1857   The squalid conditions of the Five Points leads to the deadly "Dead Rabbits Riot."

William Tecumseh Sherman moves his young family to New York City in an unsuccessful attempt to manage a Wall Street bank.

Samuel Clemens starts his two year apprentice-ship to become a river pilot on the Mississippi.

1859   November 23, Henry McCarty (a.k.a. Billy the Kid) is born in New York City.

The Cooper Union is founded.

1860   Presidential candidate Abraham Lincoln delivers a well-received speech at the Cooper Union and is elected President.

Josephine Marcus, future companion of Wyatt Earp, is born in New York City.

1861–   The nation is engulfed in a prolonged Civil War.
1865   In 1863, New York's poor immigrant Irish population reacts to President Lincoln's call for a military draft by rioting.

1866   The American Hotel closes its doors.

Long drive of cattle begins from Texas and Nebraska railheads.

On April 13, Robert Leroy Parker (a.k.a. Butch Cassidy) is born in Utah.

Frank and Jesse James rob their first bank in Liberty, Missouri.

Mark Twain begins lecturing.

1867   December, Mark Twain meets his future wife, Olivia, at the St. Nicholas Hotel.

1868   Chief Red Cloud signs a peace treaty with General William Tecumseh Sherman.

U.S. Grant narrowly wins presidency.

1869   July 21, Wild Bill Hickok kills a man in a classic gunfight on the streets of Springfield, Missouri.

Central Pacific and Union Pacific Railroads joined at Promontory Summit, Utah.

Mark Twain's first book, *The Innocents Abroad*, becomes a bestseller.

1870   Lakota Sioux Chief Red Cloud lectures at the Cooper Union.

1872   Buffalo Bill Cody visits New York City and is called upon to take a bow on the stage of the Bowery Theater.

The Gilsey House opens.

George and Libbie Custer spend the winter in New York City.

Mark Twain's *Roughing It* is published.

1873   April 1, *Scouts of the Prairie*, starring Buffalo Bill Cody, opens at Niblo's Gardens.

Later that summer, Wild Bill Hickok joins Buffalo Bill in New York City to pursue his acting career, which only lasts until early 1874, when Wild Bill returns West.

Boss Tweed is convicted of fraud and sentenced to 12 years on Blackwell's Island.

1874   June 27, Bat Masterson participates in the Battle of Adobe Walls, Texas, where two dozen buffalo hunters hold off hundreds of Comanche and Cheyenne warriors.

Jan. 24, Bat Masterson kills Army Cpl. King in a shootout in Sweetwater, TX.

1876   June 25, George Armstrong Custer and his entire command are wiped out by Sitting Bull and the Sioux on the banks of the Little Bighorn River in Montana.

July 17, Buffalo Bill exacts revenge for Custer by killing a young warrior named Yellow Hair, "taking the first scalp for Custer."

August 2, Wild Bill is shot in the back and killed while playing cards in Deadwood, North Dakota. In an effort to raise money for the Statue of Liberty's pedestal, the hand and torch were placed in Madison Square Park.

The Adventures of Tom Sawyer is published.

1877   September, Mark Twain spends an afternoon with author Robert Louis Stevenson in Washington Square Park.

Thomas Edison patents the phonograph.

Seventeen-year-old Billy the Kid shoots and kills his first man in Arizona.

1879   Madison Square Garden opens.

1881   Gunfight takes place behind the O.K. Corral in Tombstone, Arizona.

Billy the Kid killed by Pat Garrett.

P.T. Barnum and J.A. Bailey create circus known as "The Greatest Show on Earth."

1882   *Buffalo Bill's Wild West Show* begins performances. Jesse James killed by Robert Ford in St. Joseph, Missouri. Later that year, Ford and his brother would reenact the killing on Broadway.

1883   The Brooklyn Bridge opens. Theodore Roosevelt makes his first trip west.

1884   Sitting Bull takes part in a theatrical performance at New York's Eden Musée.

Mark Twain forms his own publishing firm in New York City.

1885
Sitting Bull in
Cody's Wild West
from June – October

1886   *Buffalo Bill's Wild West* plays Madison Square Garden for the first time.

Retired General William Sherman moves to New York City.

On October 28, President Grover Cleveland dedicates the Statue of Liberty.

1890 Ellis Island replaces Castle Gardens as the Federal Immigration Center.

Massacre of Sioux at Wounded Knee marks the last major clash between Native Americans and Whites.

Gen. Fremont dies in New York City.

Dec. 15, Sitting Bull is killed by Indian Police at Standing Rock Reservation in South Dakota.

1891 General William Sherman dies in his New York City townhouse.

1892 Robert Ford is killed in Creede, Colorado.

1895 May 6, Theodore Roosevelt is sworn in as a New York City Police Commissioner.

Niblo's Gardens closes.

1900 September 19, Butch Cassidy and the Sundance Kid perform their last bank robbery together on American soil in Winnemucca, Nevada.

Mark Twain moves to New York City.

1901 In February, Butch Cassidy, the Sundance Kid, and his companion, Etta Place, visit New York City.

1902 From April into July, the Sundance Kid and Etta Place again visit New York City.

On June 6, Bat Masterson is arrested in New York City. Masterson moves to the city later in the year.

In July, Pat Garrett visits New York City.

1904 New York City's first subway line opens.

1905 On December 5, a gala 70th birthday party is held for Mark Twain at Delmonico's.

Bat Masterson is appointed U.S. Marshal for the Southern District of New York.

1908   Fifth Avenue Hotel is demolished.

On February 29, Pat Garrett is shot and killed in New Mexico.

In November Butch Cassidy and the Sundance Kid are gunned down by soldiers in San Vicente, Bolivia.

1910   On April 21, Mark Twain dies.

On November 27, Pennsylvania Station opens.

1913   The Astor Hotel closes its doors.

Woolworth Building opens.

1917   On January 10, Buffalo Bill Cody dies in Colorado.

Later in the year, the United States declares war on Germany, entering World War I.

1921   On October 25, Bat Masterson dies at his desk at a New York City newspaper.

1924   Libbie Custer moves to New York City.

1929   The Bowery Theater burns down for the sixth and final time.

New York's stock market crashes throwing the country into the Great Depression.

The Waldorf Astoria is demolished to make way for construction of the Empire State Building.

Wyatt Earp dies in Los Angeles at the age of 80.

1933   Libbie Custer dies in her New York City apartment.

The Lone Ranger begins a 21-year run on ABC radio.

NYC MAP

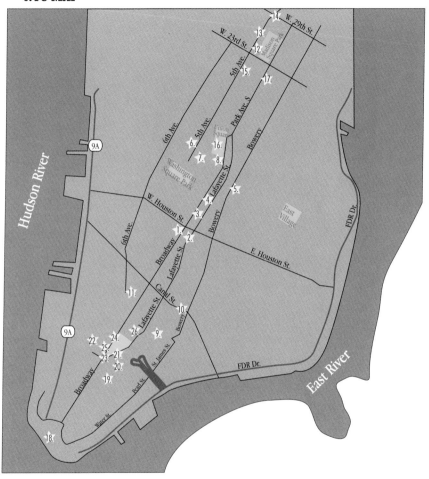

1. St. Nicholas Hotel 1853-1884
2. Niblos Garden 1823-1895
3. Pfaff's Beer Cellar
4. Grand Central Hotel 1870-1973
5. The Cooper Union 1859
6. 14 W. 10th St. Mark Twain Residence 1900-1901
7. Brevoot House Hotel
8. Hotel Albert 1887
9. Five Points
10. Bowery Theatre
11. 359 Broadway Old Brady Studio
12. Fifth Ave. Hotel 1859-1908
13. Hoffman House 1864-1895

14. Gilsey House 1871
15. Union Club 1836-1903
16. Tiffany's 1870-1905
17. The Players
18. Castle Garden
19. Delmonico's
20. 1842 Market Exchange at 55 Wall St.
21. Park Theater 1798-1848
22. Dr. Mott's Office
23. Astor House Hotel 1836-1913
24. Peale's Museum 1825-1840
25. American Hotel 1825-1866
26. Tweed Courthouse 1881

Horace Greeley statue located in City Hall Park

INTRODUCTION

"Go West, young man, and grow up with the country."
HORACE GREELEY, 1850

In 1803, President Thomas Jefferson doubled the size of the infant United States with the $15 million purchase of 800,000 square miles of land stretching from the Mississippi River to the Rocky Mountains. The following year Jefferson dispatched Meriwether Lewis and William Clark on a two-year excursion to explore the unknown territory. Upon the return of their Corps of Discovery, Americans were exposed to journals, maps, and drawings vividly depicting the natural, rugged beauty of the newly acquired land. The world's fascination with the American West had begun.

The hardships to be overcome in settling the West over the next hundred years, and the virtues required to do so, would come to define us as Americans. The Western expansion of the United States during the nineteenth century coincided with the mass publications of newspapers, almanacs, and dime novels, all of which chronicled to a receptive audience the daring deeds of frontiersmen, gunfighters, lawmen, and outlaws.

The ending of the Wild West coincided with the dawn of a new medium: moving pictures. But the advent of the new technology didn't erode the public's fascination with tales from the American West. In fact, the first plot-based movie ever filmed was a Western—*The Great Train Robbery*. Throughout the twentieth century, the Western remained the most popular genre of book, play, television series, and motion picture. The heroes and villains of the Wild West are firmly ingrained in the American culture.

What is not generally known is that many of the legendary figures of the Old West found themselves at one time or another in New York City, throughout history, as it is today, the media and culture capital of the nation. Western figures like Bat Masterson, Libbie Custer, and Mark Twain spent significant periods of time in the Big Apple. Others, like Butch Cassidy, the Sundance Kid, Buffalo Bill Cody, and David Crockett, only passed through, but the time they spent in the city had a crucial impact not only on their lives but also on the history of the young nation.

Having been raised on Western movies and television shows, I have always had a fascination with the Old West. Whenever traveling in the American West, I always make it a point to check out locations that are associated with Western figures. I never thought to look in my own backyard.

I was born in New York City, partially raised in New York City, educated in New York City, and spent significant time working in New York City, yet I was unaware that Western history pulsed all around me.

This book, however, is not a history book. I do not pretend to be a historian. The chapters you are about to read discuss New York City locations that are associated with some of the most well-known personalities of the Wild West. Hopefully, you won't be too disappointed to discover that some of the landmark buildings no longer exist. For instance, The Astor Hotel on Broadway, across from City Hall, at one time hosted an array of historical figures, from Sam Houston to Abraham Lincoln, but was demolished in 1926. Where it stood now sits a row of nondescript retail establishments that reveal no hint of the property's interesting pedigree.

The demolition of The Astor Hotel was just "progress"— doing away with the old to make room for the new, the sweeping away of a building with impressive historical significance little more than an unintended but necessary consequence of the ongoing evolution of New York City. Constant change has always been part of New York City's rich fabric. In 1839, one-time New York City mayor and dedicated diarist Philip Hone gloomily noted, "that the whole of New York is rebuilt about once in ten years."

To be sure, this observation has outlived its observer. Some of the razing was purposeful, such as the complete elimination of the infamous Five Points intersection, which Col. David Crockett toured in 1834. New York City planners successfully wiped the notorious crossing from the map by the end of the nineteenth century, and its geographical location is now Columbus Park, but tenement buildings dating to the 1820s still surround the land. Battery Park, which through the centuries has been everything from a park to a fort to an immigration center to a beer garden, provides yet another example of the perpetually shifting metropolitan landscape. Although the buildings that rose from these grounds may be gone, the locations themselves remain part of the Big Apple's history.

Fortunately, though, some of the original structures have survived into the twenty-first century, although their histories remain largely unknown to current occupants. The Elmsford Arms Apartments on 48th Street, Bat Masterson's last residence, still functions as an apartment complex. When I visited the apartment house in 2014, the lobby security officer wasn't quite sure who Bat Masterson was—he thought I was talking about Wyatt Earp—but he was quick to point out that some of the Radio City Hall Rockettes used to live in the building.

The information presented here is as accurate as I can determine. In researching the book, it was not uncommon to find conflicting facts, even between reputable historians. It's the nature of the beast. The storytelling of the American West, from the very beginning, has been an entertaining mixture of fact and fiction. As noted by a character in the John Ford classic *The Man Who Shot Liberty Valance*, "This is the West, sir. When the legend becomes fact, print the legend."

It turns out there is even some historical debate over whether Horace Greeley actually wrote the famous quotation that provides this introduction's epigraph. Its true source may be the stuff of legend, but that Horace Greeley, a New Yorker, founded and edited *The New York Tribune* is indisputable fact. And where his Tribune Building once stood now homes One Pace Plaza in lower Manhattan. There is also no debate over the the appropriate location of Greeley's statue in City Hall Park, where the monument unambiguously credits Greeley's editorials with promoting Western expansion.

Enjoy the book. Saddle up and get ready to discover the Wild West in the Big Apple.

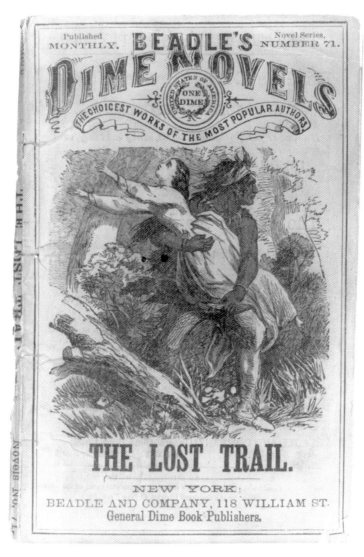

1864 Dime novel from New York's Beadle and Company (Courtesy of Library of Congress LC-USZ62-75779).

David Crockett (Print courtesy of Library of Congress LC-USZ62-7368).

DAVID CROCKETT

"I forgot I was in a City where you may live, as they tell me, years and not know who lives next door to you."
DAVID CROCKETT, 1834

On April 27, 1834, when the Honorable David Crockett, the 47-year-old Congressman from Tennessee, stepped off of the Steamboat *New Philadelphia* and onto the streets of New York City, he was arguably the most famous man in the United States.

What had propelled him into the national spotlight and into the Port of New York was a uniquely American series of events.

Davy Crockett, as every baby boomer surely knows thanks to the famous theme song, was born on a mountaintop in Tennessee. What is less well-known: the year was 1786, and the location was a log cabin in the State of Franklin, part of North Carolina and destined eventually to become the State of Tennessee. Nevertheless, David, as he preferred to be called, lived the vast majority of his life in the wilderness of the Volunteer State.

As a boy, he was hired out to farmers and drovers to pay off his father's never-ending stream of debt. His father constantly uprooted the family for the sake of different business ventures. The Crocketts ran a mill, farmed, and operated a tavern, all with the same disastrous financial results.

Young David honed his skills as a hunter and developed a friendly, optimistic personality. Perhaps from his time at the family tavern, he also acquired a knack for conversation and the telling of tall tales.

By the age of 20, he was married and scratching out a living in East Tennessee. He volunteered to fight Indians in the Creek War under General Andrew Jackson, and Crockett's ability to bring in fresh game made him a popular comrade in arms.

His life, to an extent, was typical for a son of the frontier. He certainly experienced his share of hardships. Shortly after returning from the Creek War, his young wife, Polly, died suddenly, leaving David alone to raise three small children. He quickly remarried a widow, Elizabeth Patton, who had two children of her own. Their marriage was strained, at best, but they would have three more children together.

Like his father before him, David embarked on a series of business ventures, all of which were destined for the same fate. He invested $3,000, Elizabeth's funds and borrowed money, in a gristmill, distillery, and gunpowder factory, but the sum was lost when the Shoal Creek flooded. Similarly, he lost an investment in riverboats when two vessels loaded with timber for barrels sunk in the Mississippi, with David aboard.

As for farming, David was simply not an agriculturist. He much preferred to be out hunting, at which, even by frontier standards, he excelled. He single-handedly depleted the bear population of West Tennessee by 105 in one hunting season alone.

Also like his father, David repeatedly moved his ever-growing family westward across Tennessee in search of new land, new opportunities, and an escape from old debts. Along the way, he discovered a profession that came to him as naturally as hunting: politics. He could deliver a humorous speech as well as anyone, and he relished sharing a few "horns" in the local tavern, where the storytelling inevitably continued. In his homespun yarns, he was usually the hapless hero, the man who somehow managed to emerge victorious from his frontier adventures. Naturally, people liked him, and his neighbors admired his frontier skills. He became a Justice of the Peace and was later elected Colonel of the Lawrence County, Tennessee, Militia. Henceforth, he would be referred to as Col. Crockett.

In 1821, he was elected to the Tennessee State Legislature, where he gained a reputation for sticking up for settlers by seeking to maintain reasonable land prices. Crockett identified with the "common man" and felt it was his obligation to look out for their interests. He overcame his lack of education and his limited knowledge of legislative procedure with his self-effacing humor. He served two terms before deciding, in 1825, to run for Congress. He was narrowly defeated.

Never a quitter, David ran again in 1827. This time, he won a seat in the Twentieth United States Congress. Crockett took Washington by storm. He was the proverbial fish out of water, and the press ate up his colorful antics and folksy speeches. But he was more than a source of entertainment. He was self-educated, self-reliant, and unafraid to speak his mind. In retrospect, he was the embodiment of the American frontier. Crockett would lose another election in 1831, but he would be elected to a second term in 1833, much to the delight of the national press.

By the time Crockett returned to Congress, a two-act play had opened in New York City, entitled *The Lion of the West*. The farce's main character, a coonskin-cap-wearing colonel named Nimrod Wildfire, was little more than a thinly disguised David Crockett. Wildfire's dialogue, in some instances, came right from exaggerated newspaper quotes supposedly sourced from Crockett himself. There was no doubt in the public's mind that Col. Nimrod Wildfire was none other than Col. David Crockett. The wild popularity of the play inspired a series of books and so-called biographies of Crockett, the first of which, *Sketches and Eccentricities of Colonel David Crockett*, was published in 1833. The book utilized quotes from Crockett but also incorporated dialogue from Col. Nimrod. The mythical Davy Crockett had arrived.

In 1833, Crockett attended a performance of *The Lion of the West* in Washington, and, as brilliantly captured in the 2004 film *The Alamo*, stood in the audience and bowed to Col. Nimrod, who himself returned the gesture, the man and the character acknowledging each other directly for the first time. Myth and fact had merged into a legend in a coonskin cap, and there would be no looking back.

Outwardly, Crockett enjoyed his celebrity, but privately he couldn't believe that everybody appeared to be making money on Davy Crockett except David Crockett himself, who still struggled beneath a Tennessee mountain of debt. It wasn't Crockett's nature to be bitter, but neither was it his nature to sit back and do nothing. He wrote his own book: *A Narrative of the Life of David Crockett of the State of Tennessee*. He said he wrote the book to set the record straight concerning the misconceptions being written about him. However, his version was filled with its own exaggerated examples of his hunting prowess, as well as questionable tales of his heroic participation in Indian battles. Yet he also discussed his various business follies honestly, doing so in a homespun, folksy manner that the public ate up. The entire country knew his motto: "Be Sure you're right— then Go Ahead." Although he clearly had help writing the book, the humor is pure Crockett. His down-to-earth voice, sprinkled with frontier expressions, established a style that would be copied and built upon by future American humorists like Mark Twain and Will Rogers. Crockett's book is still in print today.

Crockett also used the memoir for political purposes, jabbing at President Andrew Jackson. One would think Crockett had been a protégé of Old Hickory. Both were, after all, "common men" from the Western frontier of Tennessee. Crockett had even served under then-General Jackson in the Creek War. Crockett, however, had a severe flaw for a politician: integrity. He sincerely believed that it was his sworn duty to represent his constituents from the wilds of Tennessee. For the duration of his time in Congress, Crockett unsuccessfully attempted to pass a land bill that would have allowed poor settlers to maintain ownership of the land on which they had been squatting, instead of the land being made available to Eastern developers. This stance was in direct conflict with Jackson's vision of the

United States' continuous Western expansion to the Pacific Ocean, a concept later termed "Manifest Destiny."

Crockett's final break with Jacksonian Democrats resulted from his very vocal opposition to Jackson's Indian Removal Act, which would remove all Native Americans living east of the Mississippi to a newly defined Indian Territory in present day Oklahoma. He explained in his autobiography that he opposed the bill "from the purest motives in the world … [I]t was a wicked unjust measure … ." Needless to say, the Indian Removal Act passed despite Crockett's harsh criticism. The resulting relocation along the 1,000-mile-long Trail of Tears led to the deaths of thousands of men, women, and children of the Cherokee, Muscogee, Seminole, Chickasaw, and Choctaw nations.

Crockett's rising popularity, and his widening divide with Jackson, was not lost on members of the new Whig party, which had formed in opposition to President Jackson's policies expanding the authority of the Executive Branch. Crockett was courted by the Whigs as a possible presidential candidate in 1836. In 1834, while Congress was still in session, Crockett's new Whig friends convinced him to go on a three week junket of the Northeast. The Whigs saw the tour as an opportunity to have the famous frontiersman publicly bash Jackson, and to gauge Crockett's chances for a run at the Executive Mansion. Crockett saw the opportunity to sell more books. In the carefully orchestrated boondoggle, Crockett would ride a train for the first time, be wined and dined by politicians, newspaper editors, book publishers, military leaders, and a curious public in cities like Baltimore, Philadelphia, Newport, Boston, Lowell, Providence, Camden, and, of course, New York.

The American Hotel

An enthusiastic crowd met the Honorable David Crockett at the Port of New York and led him up Broadway to his accommodations at The American Hotel. Located at 229-233 Broadway, on the corner of Barclay Street, the hotel faced City Hall and City Hall Park. The hotel was built in 1825, and its proprietor, William C. Cozzens, would go on to build the Cozzens Hotel, the first hotel at West Point. At the time, it was the

Contemporary photo of Woolworth Building, The Cathedral of Commerce

finest in the city and could accommodate 400 guests. Other famous guests to stay at the hotel before Crockett included his nemesis, Andrew Jackson, and Whig friend Henry Clay.

The American Hotel closed its doors in 1866. Today, the site is occupied by the Woolworth Building, itself an architectural marvel. At the Woolworth's opening in April 1913, almost 50 years after The American Hotel shuttered its doors, and 80 years since it welcomed Crockett, New Yorkers were astonished when President Wilson, pressing a button in Washington, lit 80,000 bulbs in New York. The 57-story Gothic Revival-style skyscraper was the tallest building in the world until the opening of the Chrysler Building in 1929. One wonders if Crockett could have imagined such things as he approached his lodging all those years before.

Contemporary photo of entrance to Woolworth Building. (What would Col. Crockett do if confronted with this greeting in 1834?)

Astor House Hotel, Broadway, 1867 (Print courtesy of Library of Congress LC DIG- 05-01872).

Just south of The American Hotel, between Vesey and Barclay Streets, another landmark lodging would make its home. Though he never stayed there, Crockett surely noticed the on-going construction of the Astor House Hotel. Financed by John Jacob Astor, the six-story building opened in June 1836 and was christened the Park Hotel. It had over 300 rooms, was lit by gaslight, and had indoor plumbing. In its heyday, it was the most luxurious hotel in America

Photo of the 1913 Auction (Courtesy of the Museum of the City of New York).

Broadway and Vesey today.

17

and housed such famous guests as Sam Houston, Henry Wadsworth Longfellow, Matthew Brady, Charles Dickens, James Garfield, James Polk, Daniel Webster, Jefferson Davis, and Abraham Lincoln (the latter two at different times). In 1848, the cost of a room was $2 a day, and lunch was free.

Sadly, in 1913, due in part to family squabbles among the Astors, the hotel furnishings were auctioned off and the hotel was demolished (see page 16). Another piece of American history was lost.

Crockett paid the 25-cent admission fee and visited Peale's Museum, located at 252 Broadway in an ornate building called the Pantheon. The museum was owned and operated by Rubens Peale, the son of the famous artist, Charles Wilson Peale. The museum showcased "curiosities and Freaks" the likes of which Crockett had never seen. He was amazed by the Siamese twins; a boy without arms, but who handled scissors with his toes, a 300-pound Kentucky strongman, Egyptian mummies, and ventriloquists. New Yorkers were anxious to catch a glimpse of the wild man from the west, a creature who was "half horse, half alligator, and a little touched with the snapping turtle."

Crockett's attendance at the museum was noted in a young woman's letter home:

> I went to Peale's Museum last evening and saw many wonderful things of course … But what will interest you the most of all probably … is that I have seen a great man. No less of one than Col. Crockett. I … sat close by him so I had a good opportunity of observing his physiognomy … He is wholly different than what I thought him. Tall in stature and large in frame, but quite thin, with

black hair combed straight over the forehead, parted
from the middle and his shirt collar turned negligently
over his coat. He has rather a indolent and careless
appearance and does not look like a "go ahead" man …

Peale eventually sold his entire collection in 1840 to
P.T. Barnum, who opened the Barnum's American Museum
on the corner of Broadway and Ann Street.

Peale's Museum, 1825 (Courtesy of the Museum of the City of New York).

252 Broadway today.

THE FIVE POINTS

In 1834, the most notorious neighborhood in the United States, if not the world, was the Five Points section of lower Manhattan. The five-pointed intersection of Anthony (now Worth), Orange (now Baxter), Cross, and Little Water Streets created a triangular block, forming a point. Crockett made the short walk from The American Hotel on Broadway up Pearl Street to tour the infamous Five Points.

In the 1820s and '30s, a variety of socio-economic factors led to the neighborhood's devolution to an overcrowded, disease-ridden slum—not the least of which was the rush of Irish immigration, which in the late 1820s was estimated at over 30,000 people per year. The immigrants found cheap housing in the decrepit buildings that had been subdivided into rooms wherein as many unfortunate souls as possible could be squeezed. These ramshackle residences ultimately evolved into tenement housing. Crockett, perhaps blissfully unaware of his own Irish ancestry, commented thusly with regard to the Irish immigrants: "[They are] worse than savages; they are too mean to swab hell's kitchen."

In 1834, the Five Points also housed a significant number of African Americans who openly mixed with Whites, a situation that did not go unnoticed by the Southern Crockett. He noted, "Black and White, White and Black, all hugemsnug together, happy as lords and ladies, sitting sometimes round in a ring, with a jug of liquor between them; and I do think I saw more drunk folks, men and women, that day than I ever saw before ..."

In addition to the deplorable housing and the unsanitary conditions, the Five Points was rampant with saloons, beer joints, and brothels. Fueled by alcohol, the Five Points

Five Points by George Catlin, 1827

What is left of the infamous Five Points intersection today looking down Moska Street into Mulberry Street.

was a hotbed of tension between native-born Americans and immigrants, Catholics and Protestants, and abolitionists and anti-abolitionists. The Five Points was also the birthplace of such storied gangs as the Dead Rabbits, the Bowery Boys, the Plug Uglies, the Short Tails, the Slaughter Houses, the Swamp Angels, and the Mulberry Boys. Just two months after Crockett's visit, a four-day riot raged in the Five Points, pitting anti-abolitionists against African Americans and their abolitionist allies.

It was a dangerous place, to be sure. Assaults, robberies, and muggings were commonplace. Charles Dickens would call the Five-Points "a place of vice and misery." Crockett observed, with a touch of both sincerity and truth, "I thought I would rather risque myself in an Indian fight than venture among these creatures after night."

Crockett, who spent a lifetime moving westward across the vast American landscape, from Tennessee to homesteads on new land, was dumbstruck by the crowded living conditions. "There are more people stowed away together here," Crockett noted, "than any place I ever saw … I sometimes wonder they don't clear out to a new country … ."

The Five Points would continue to deteriorate over the next half century. Irish immigrants would continue to pour in, a result of the Irish Potato Famine in the 1840s. The slum would continue to serve as an overcrowded host to

65 Mott Street, New York's first tenement built in 1824.

new generations of immigrants—Germans, Jews, Italians, and Chinese—and the rampant crime, prostitution, political graft, and gang warfare would drag on. In 1857, the Dead Rabbits Riot between rival gangs the Dead Rabbits and the Bowery Boys resulted in over twenty deaths.

By the time of the Civil War, the population of the Five Points had begun to decrease. Social reform and, ultimately, the building of municipal buildings helped mark the end of the Five Points. Today, the Civic Center encompasses the western and southern boundary of what was the Five Points, and what is left of Little Italy and Chinatown form the eastern and northern boundaries. Today, you will search in vain for the five-pointed intersection, the once-notorious location replaced, for the most part, by Columbus Park. The geographic location of the infamous intersection is the crossing of Worth and Baxter Streets. However, a walk through Chinatown today will reveal that some of the original tenements are still standing, a reminder of what once had been when Crockett wound the same route.

The Bowery Theater

Crockett had to be persuaded to attend a performance of *The Tragedy of King Lear* starring Junius Brutus Booth at the rowdy Bowery Theater, located at 46 Bowery. The New York newspapers had advertised Crockett's attendance, so he reluctantly agreed to go. The freewheeling, burlesque-type atmosphere made it not only a Five Points favorite, but one of the most preferred venues in of all New York. Prostitutes openly solicited willing patrons in the balcony, and the 3,000 seat theater was nationally known as "the worst and wickedest."

Drawn by C.Burton.   Engraved by H.Fossette.

BOWERY THEATRE,

NEW YORK.

New York,BOURNE,Broadway.

"Entered according to the Act of Congress in the year 1831 by G.MELKSEAM BOURNE, in the Clerks Office of the District court of the Southern District of New York."

Bowery Theater drawn by C. Burton, 1828.

The Bowery Theatre was constructed in 1826 on the site of the old New York cattle yards, which adjoined the Bulls Head Tavern, a favorite watering hole of George Washington. Despite its sordid reputation, the Bowery Theatre owned an impressive theatrical pedigree. From the 1820s through the 1850s, the most prominent actor of his era, Junius Brutus Booth, would perform Shakespeare to an admiring audience, a mix of the young nation's elite and the Five Points ruffians. Walt Whitman, James Fenimore Cooper, Andrew Jackson, Martin Van Buren, and William Tyler were among the thespian's fans.

26

46 Bowery today. Note the old building with the dormers on the left.

The Bowery Theater would go on to host boisterous vaudeville and Black-face minstrel shows. It burned down for the sixth and final time in 1929, and today the site is occupied by the Jing Fong Chinese Restaurant.

A decade after the rarely sober Junius Brutus Booth performed on the Bowery Theater stage, his son John Wilkes Booth met with fellow conspirators at Mary Surratt's Washington D.C. boarding house, located at 604 H Street, and plotted the assassination of President Abraham Lincoln. The fate of this Booth family landmark proved more fortunate than the Bowery Theater. The structure still stands, the site occupied, like that of the old Bowery, by a Chinese restaurant, the Wok and Roll. God Bless America—easy on the MSG.

The Park Theatre

Crockett attended a performance at the Park Theater, on Chatham St., across from City Hall, which is now located at 21, 23, and 25 Park Row. The Park Theater opened for business in 1798, and originally catered to an upscale clientele. It was initially the "New Theater," and until the early 1820s was New York's only theater.

On April 25, 1831, *The Lion of the West* opened at the Park Theater. It would go on to be the most performed American play until the run of *Uncle Tom's Cabin*, which premiered in 1852, unseated it.

By the 1840s, the Park Theater had seen better days, and then-theater critic Edgar Allan Poe noted that the rats came out "on cue" when the curtain rose, scouring for peanuts and orange peels.

It is unlikely that a few rats would have bothered the King of the Wild Frontier, and Crockett thoroughly enjoyed

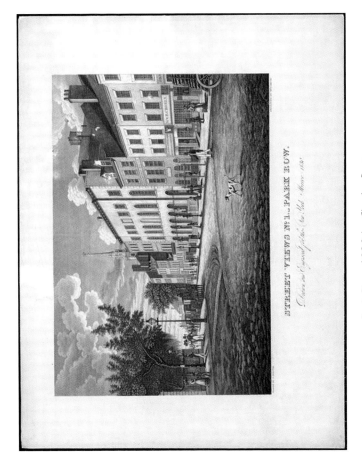

Park Row, 1830 by Charles Burton.

29

Park Row today.

the performance. He noted that the star of the show, famed British actress Fanny Kemble, was "like a handsome piece of changeable silk; first one color then another, but always the clean thing."

The Park Theater burned down in 1848, and owner John Jacob Astor decided not to rebuild, choosing instead to construct stores.

City Hall

Col. Crockett walked from his hotel across Broadway through City Hall Park. He met Mayor Gideon Lee and found the mayor to be a "plain, common sense looking man." New York's City Hall was completed in 1812, and Crockett noted that while the front of the building was marble, the rear, which faced the Poor House, was brownstone. Crockett surmised that this disparity symbolized the Jacksonian Democrat's distaste for common people.

City Hall and Broadway, 1825 (Courtesy of the Museum of the City of New York).

City Hall today.

In any event, although City Hall has gone through numerous renovations over the years, including replacing both the marble and brownstone with limestone, it stands today as the oldest operating city hall in the United States.

Battery Park

Col. Crockett was brought to Battery Park on the southern tip of Manhattan, which was the original site of a seventeenth century Dutch fort. The old fort was razed in 1788, and landfill was added to extend the area to about 10 acres. By the time of Crockett's visit, a new circular fort named Castle Clinton had been constructed for use as a public park. There, Crockett observed a military ceremony in which a new flag was hoisted onto the same flagstaff as the British Union Jack had been taken down from when the British evacuated Manhattan on November 25, 1783, a date celebrated as a national holiday for over a hundred years before being replaced by Thanksgiving. Legend has it that prior to leaving New York, the British left the Union Jack flying and greased the pole. The Americans had difficulty taking down the flag until an enterprising sailor, using wooden cleats, tore down the British banner and raised the Stars and Stripes.

Crockett was impressed with the park and the ceremony, which included Revolutionary War veterans. He noted that it was "a beautiful meadow of a place, all measured off with nice walks of gravel between the grass plats, full of big shade trees, filled with people and a great many children that come there to get the fresh air that comes off the water of the bay."

National Park Service rendering of Castle Clinton in the 1830s.

The Battery also encompassed Castle Garden, America's first beer garden. Over the years, Crockett, on several occasions, had promised his wife that he would abstain from alcohol. However, by this time, Crockett's wife had left him, so the Congressman was free to partake fully in the festivities. He noted that "[n]obody thinks anything well done in this place, without eating and drinking over it."

Over the years, numerous receptions and performances were held at Castle Garden, but between 1855 and 1890, it was utilized as a Federal Immigration Center. Clipper ships, including the *David Crockett*, would deposit over 8 million immigrants onto Castle Garden. In 1890, Ellis Island replaced Castle Garden, and the building was turned over to New York City. The New York Aquarium was operated there from 1896 until 1941.

Entrance to Castle Clinton today.

35

Today, Battery Park is a 25-acre park operated by the City of New York and the National Park Service. It is a beautifully landscaped park with breathtaking views. Monuments and memorials line the grounds as well. It also is an active harbor, servicing ferries to Staten Island, Ellis Island, and the Statute of Liberty.

The Market Exchange
The famous backwoodsman was escorted to the Market Exchange, which he described as "the place where the merchants assemble every day at one o'clock, to hear all they can, and tell as little as possible; and where two lines from a knowing correspondent prudently used, may make a fortune." With a little prodding, Crockett made another anti-Jackson speech on the steps of the old Market Exchange Building, which was located at 55 Wall Street. The New York Evening Star reported that Crockett "delivered a few short and pithy sentences in his quaint and original style."

The first organized stock market in New York was formed on May 17, 1792, under a buttonwood tree at what is now 68 Wall Street.

The Merchants Exchange Building burned down in the great fire of December 1835, which destroyed approximately 700 buildings in lower Manhattan. The normally efficient volunteer firemen couldn't control the blaze because the fire hydrants and hoses froze in the sub-zero temperatures.

The rebuilding of the Market Exchange took place between 1836 and 1842. It became the New York Customs House in 1863 when the Stock Exchange moved to a new location. Today, the 1842 Greek-revival-style building at 55 Wall Street has been enlarged and renovated and now

Wall Street in the early 19th Century (Courtesy of the Museum of the City of New York).

The 1842 Market Exchange at 55 Wall Street.

houses upscale apartments. Meanwhile, the New York Stock Exchange has been in its current building at 18 Broad Street since 1903.

Crockett departed New York on May 1, 1834, and continued up to New England, where his whirlwind partying continued. On May 9, he stopped back in New York for a night and seemed relieved to leave the next morning, finding New York to be a "city of eternal din and confusion." Crockett made it out of New York unscathed, although he couldn't say the same about his time in New Jersey, a Camden pickpocket having nabbed from Crockett $150. Davy Crockett would never go back to New York; he had less than two years to live.

Crockett returned to Washington to find his political luster beginning to wear thin. His well-publicized sojourn through the Northeast had caused him to miss some important sessions of Congress, and his beloved land bill was going nowhere. Pro-Jackson newspapers were highly critical of Crockett, calling him a "buffoon," and claiming he lost $1,500 gambling while on his tour of the Northeast.

Crockett's verbal attacks on Jackson and Martin Van Buren, the apparent presidential successor, became more numerous and vicious. It riled Crockett that Jackson could seemingly appoint his successor, which to Crockett smacked of a European monarchy. Crockett threatened to leave the country if Van Buren was elected in 1836.

Crockett faced an election of his own in August 1835, but he spent an inordinate amount of time criticizing "King Andrew" and Van Buren instead of attending to his congressional duties. In fact, he collaborated on two books in which he received author credit: one discussing his Northeast tour and the other a libelous assault on Van Buren, the latter awkwardly titled *The Life of Martin Van Buren, Heir-apparent to the Government and the Appointed Successor of General Jackson.*

Crockett narrowly lost his bid for reelection. Although political chips clearly were stacked against him, historians cite Crockett's Northeast tour as a major factor in his defeat.

Prior to leaving Washington, Crockett spent some time cavorting with fellow Tennessee eccentric Sam Houston, who was extolling Texas's potential as a land of new opportunity. Americans, for years, had been pouring into the Mexican Province of Texas, and relations between the Texans and their Mexican rulers were reaching a boiling point. It was manifest destiny that Americans were to have Texas, and that Texas would have Davy Crockett.

In the fall of 1835, the lame-duck Congressman told Tennessee voters that "they might all go to hell and [he] will go to Texas." Upon his arrival in Texas, where Col. Crockett hoped to find a fresh start, he took an oath of allegiance to the newly formed provisional government and soon found himself among the 189 volunteers in San Antonio. The Texas defenders had fortified a century-old Spanish mission called the Alamo and were awaiting the inevitable arrival of General Antonio Lopez de Santa Anna, who, along with his 4,000 troops, was determined to quash the Texas rebellion.

When Crockett arrived at the Alamo, he brought with him about a dozen volunteers he had picked up along the way. The defenders' spirits were immediately uplifted. In their midst was the most famous man in America. But Crockett wasn't there only to rally the men and observe events from the sidelines. He informed co-Commanders William Barret Travis and James Bowie that he wanted to serve as a "high private."

Among the defenders were six native New Yorkers, and five others who at one time or another had lived in New York. New York City records reveal that one defender, Lewis Dewall, was living at 51 Lewis Street, on the Lower East Side, in 1833.

Crockett meshed well with the frontier defenders, whom he kept entertained with fiddle playing, tall tales, and jokes about Santa Anna. Travis's letters and recollections from the non-combatant survivors of the battle all paint an image of Crockett as a man who had a powerful and positive impact on the morale of the Texans during the 13-day siege. According to Travis, Crockett "was seen at all points animating the men to do their duty."

Col. Crockett and his men had been assigned to defend the southeast side of the compound, which was protected only by a low wooden palisade. Upon being given this perilous assignment, Crockett assured Col. Travis that "[he] and [his] Tennessee boys [would] defend it."

In the pre-dawn hours of March 6, 1836, Santa Anna launched an all-out assault on the Alamo, promising to leave no survivors. Crockett was true to his word, and, although it was the most exposed portion of the compound, the palisade was never breached. The Mexicans soon burst through the north wall, however, and swept through the Alamo. The ill-fated path through life that had led Crockett and his fellow defenders to the Alamo had been one in which every adversity had been met head on, often with violent consequences. These men were adventurers, bear hunters, and Indian fighters who did not go gently into that good night. They exacted a heavy toll on the advancing troops, using Bowie knives, rifle butts, tomahawks, and fists in their desperate but losing struggle. Ninety minutes after the final assault began, one of the most heroic battles ever fought on American soil was over. Santa Anna ordered the bodies of the 189 defenders burned, a final show of disrespect.

Six weeks after the fall of the Alamo, Santa Anna would be routed by Sam Houston and his fledgling army, amid cries of "Remember the Alamo," in the somewhat bizarre 18-minute battle of San Jacinto. Houston and his men caught the self-proclaimed "Napoleon of the West" and his army taking a siesta at 3:30 in the afternoon, and just like that the Texas War for Independence was won.

Clearly, the most famous casualty of the battle of the Alamo was Col. David Crockett. The details surrounding Crockett's death have always been a source of controversy. Some contemporaries refused to believe that the seemingly indestructible Davy Crockett could have perished. Newspapers, for years afterward, would publish accounts of supposed Crockett sightings, including a report that Crockett was a Mexican prisoner working in a mine.

There is no historical doubt that Col. Crockett perished during the siege of the Alamo. According to Travis's slave, Joe, who was among the fortunate non-combatant survivors, "Crockett and a few of his friends were found together with 24 of the enemy dead around them." Similarly, Mrs. Susannah Dickinson, the 15-year-old wife of Capt. Dickinson, recalled seeing Crockett's body by the Alamo Chapel, with "his peculiar hat" at his side. Even so, the unanswered question remains: "How did Davy die?"

The historical controversy surrounding Crockett's death reached a feverish pitch in 1975, when an English translation of a Mexican officer's "diary" was published. The officer's record included a paragraph on Crockett's death. Alamo scholars generally agreed that at the end of the siege seven Texan combatants were taken prisoner by the Mexicans. The seven were brought before Santa Anna, who promptly ordered their executions. Lt. Colonel José Enrique de la Pena's diary, however, added a wrinkle: David Crockett had been one of those seven captives. Obviously, this scenario did not coincide with the image of Davy Crockett fighting like a tiger to the bitter end, which had been implanted into the consciousness of generations of Americans through books, television, and film. Some historians who have embraced the de la Pena diary have accused those who refuse to accept the diary as unable to let go of their childhood fantasies. Critics of the de la Pena version are quick to point out there may be severe problems with the diary's authenticity and have labeled the diary's proponents as revisionists intent on destroying one of America's most sacred legends. Whole books have been written on this subject alone by respected historians who come down on either side of the thorny issue. There is no doubt, however, in the legend's most important premise: David Crockett perished at the Alamo while fighting against overwhelming odds in the name of freedom.

The significance of the spectacular and heroic death of Davy Crockett was not lost on nineteenth-century writers. Books, almanacs, and plays featuring Davy Crockett's exploits would continue to be popular into the next century.

The popularity of the Davy Crockett legend, which always had been based on a combination of fact and fiction, assumed a new role in the American psyche when Walt Disney's *Davy Crockett* television series aired in 1955. Fess Parker's portrayal of the title character sparked a Crockett craze across the nation the likes of which have never been matched. "The Ballad of Davy Crockett" was on the Hit Parade for six months, lasting three as the number one song. Schools were renamed, and over 4,000 different Davy Crockett items, from coonskin caps to furniture, flooded a more than willing market. The timing for the revival of the Crockett legend was just right. The United States was still basking in post-World War II patriotism and prosperity, and

Col. Crockett's Method of Wading the Mississippi.

NASHVILLE, TENN. PUBLISHED FOR THE AUTHOR.

1836 Crockett Almanac (Courtesy of Library of Congress LC-USZ62-67575)

44

the heroic virtues of Disney's Crockett reminded Americans of what it would take to win the Cold War. None other than super-patriot John Wayne would play Crockett in the 1960 blockbuster *The Alamo*.

Davy Crockett remains an almost mythical figure in the American psyche. Col. David Crockett, however, was a real-life figure, perhaps the first true American celebrity. For almost 200 years, he has symbolized the virtues of honesty, bravery, and self-reliance, the values that are associated with the American West. Although far from perfect, in historical retrospect, he lived up to his legend, and in the spring of 1834 he walked the streets of New York.

The Fort Worth Photograph. The Sundance Kid is seated on the left, and Butch Cassidy is seated on the right (Courtesy of Utah State Historical Society).

BUTCH CASSIDY AND THE SUNDANCE KID

"… [I]t shows how daring these people are, while looking
for them in the mountains and the wilderness
they are in the midst of society."
ROBERT PINKERTON ON BUTCH CASSIDY
AND THE SUNDANCE KID, 1901

On February 1, 1901, Mr. and Mrs. Harry A. Place checked into Mrs. Catherine Taylor's Boarding House at 234 W. 12th St. in New York's Greenwich Village. They were soon joined in their spacious second-floor suite, which overlooked Greenwich Avenue, by Mrs. Place's brother, Mr. James Ryan. Unbeknownst to the good Mrs. Taylor, her somewhat rowdy guests were none other than the most notorious and wanted outlaws in the American West: Butch Cassidy, the Sundance Kid, and the Kid's mysterious companion, Etta Place.

Butch Cassidy was born Robert LeRoy Parker in Utah in 1866. Butch soon strayed from his Mormon roots and took to horse rustling, which landed him a year-and-a-half-long stay in the Wyoming State Penitentiary in 1894. When Cassidy left prison, he assembled a gang and turned his attention to banks and trains. His gang's reign lasted about five years and was known first as The Hole in the Wall Gang after its hideout in Kaycee, Wyoming. Later on, it would be known as The Wild Bunch.

234 West 12th Street, corner of W. 12th and Greenwich Ave. today.

Cassidy was a likable sort, for a bank robber, and bragged that he never killed anyone. Wanted posters described him as "cheery and affable." Butch and the gang liked to use dynamite to open express cars, but they would first separate the car from the rest of the train and shout a warning to any guards that might be inside.

A trusted member of The Wild Bunch, and a confidante of Butch, was Harry Alonzo Longbaugh, who was born in Pennsylvania but soon drifted west. After a stint in jail for horse stealing in Sundance, Wyoming, he would henceforth be known as the Sundance Kid. Although he was considered the gang's best shot, it is also likely he never killed anybody. In the 1969 film *Butch Cassidy and the Sundance Kid*, Paul Newman and Robert Redford perfectly captured the chivalrous personalities of the surprisingly good-natured outlaws.

Other members of the gang included Harry Tracy ("Elzy Lay"), Ben Kilpatrick ("the tall Texan"), and Harvey Logan ("Kid Curry").

Historians have estimated that The Wild Bunch earned about $200,000 by robbing trains and banks throughout South Dakota, New Mexico, Nevada, Utah, and Wyoming. In today's dollars, that sum would be over $4 million. Eastern newspapers detailed The Wild Bunch's flamboyant robberies to appreciative readers who enjoyed following the romanticized activities of the last Western outlaw band. As the nineteenth century was coming to a close, the Union Pacific Railroad had enough of The Wild Bunch and retained the services of the famed Pinkerton National Detective Agency to put an end to the costly string of train robberies. The Pinkertons were a private Detective Agency established by Allan Pinkerton in 1851, and by the late nineteenth century had become the largest private law enforcement organization in the world.

Butch Cassidy and the Sundance Kid partnered on their last heist on American soil on September 19, 1900. They duo relieved the First National Bank in Winnemucca, Nevada of more than $32,000 in gold coins. Five members of the gang, including Butch and Sundance, met up in Fort Worth, Texas and spent several weeks enjoying their ill-gotten gains. At one point in their revelry, the members of the gang sat for a portrait dressed in their Sunday best. The now-famous photograph found its way into the hands of Pinkerton Detectives, who distributed cropped versions that had been repurposed into mug shots. Prior to fingerprinting, mug shots and physical descriptions were the sole source of identification, making them a vital law enforcement tool. The boys reportedly sent a copy to the Winnemucca Bank, along with a note of thanks.

It was the beginning of the end of The Wild Bunch, and Butch and Sundance knew it. They decided they would pursue a peaceful, lawful retirement in Argentina, far out of the reach of law enforcement, especially the Pinkertons.

But Butch and Sundance, with Etta Place at his side, had one more stop to make before turning south. They would rendezvous in New York City in February 1901.

Historians still have not figured out exactly who Etta Place was. The Pinkertons considered her a full-fledged member of The Hole in the Wall Gang and haphazardly identified her as "Ethel," "Eva," and "Etta." "Place" may have been an alias, as well, since "Place" was Sundance's mother's maiden name. Despite struggling to settle on a name, the Pinkertons were nevertheless able to note that she had "classic good looks."

Speculation of her background ranges from school teacher to prostitute, and it is unclear whether she ever married Sundance, who routinely identified her as his wife. While in the big city, Butch, Sundance, and Etta played tourist, and did some shopping as well.

Tiffany's

Early in the trip, Butch, using the alias James Ryan, purchased a gold lapel watch for $40.10 from Tiffany's, which was located at the corner of 15th Street and Union Square

Corner of 15th Street and Union Square West today.

West in a large five-story cast-iron building. In 1870, Tiffany's had moved from 550 Broadway, where it had been since 1853 when it first moved from its 1847 location at 271 Broadway. In 1906, Tiffany's moved first to Fifth Avenue and 37th Street before ultimately settling into its current prestigious address at Fifth Avenue and 57th Street, where a nine-foot-tall statute of Atlas holding a round clock, taken from the 550 Broadway location, adorns the outside of the building.

The Union Square store where Butch made his purchase was converted and expanded to accommodate 36 ultra-high-end residences, which added seven new floors to the original building. The new zinc-framed glass walls sit two feet in front of the remaining 1870 cast-iron structure.

DeYoung Studio
On February 3, 1901, Sundance and Etta posed for a portrait photograph taken by Joseph DeYoung at his studio at 857 Broadway, at East 17th Street. Historians have speculated that DeYoung may have shot the infamous couple's wedding photo, and that the lapel watch worn by Etta, perhaps the same one Butch had purchased at Tiffany's, had been given to her as wedding gift from Butch. Months later the Pinkertons would interview DeYoung about the outlaws, and the photographer would tell the detectives that the pair were so well-mannered he had taken them to be "Western Society."

Despite DeYoung's favorable impression, the Pinkertons would leave the studio much more than empty-handed. They took with them a copy of the supposed wedding photo, the ramifications of which would be severe for Butch and Sundance. The Pinkertons would use the photo on wanted

DeYoung Photograph (Courtesy of Library of Congress LCUSZ62-132506)

posters that were distributed to Pinkerton agents throughout the country and, ultimately, in Buenos Aires.

St. Mark's Eye and Ear Hospital

While in the city, the Sundance Kid also sought out the services of Dr. Issac Weinstein, a physician associated with St. Mark's Eye and Ear Hospital who had an office at 174 Second Avenue. Prior to traveling to New York City, Sundance and Etta had stopped in Buffalo, New York, where Sundance sought treatment at Dr. Pierce's Invalid Hotel. According to

174 Second Avenue today.

the Pinkerton investigation, Sundance was being treated for a "pistol-shot wound he said he got in the West." It is believed, however, that Dr. Weinstein treated Sundance for an ongoing problem with his sinus.

Today, the five-story building where Dr. Weinstein once practiced houses apartments and a Chinese restaurant.

Buenos Aires

On February 20, 1901, the hard-partying trio left New York bound for Buenos Aires on the British steamer Herminius. They arrived in Buenos Aires on March 23, determined to start a new life as law-abiding ranchers. They settled in Cholila, Argentina, and began purchasing land and horses.

54

New York City 1902

Sundance and Etta returned to New York City on April 3, 1902, leaving Butch in Argentina to work on ranch business. The Pinkertons later speculated that Etta was homesick, but the pair may have had medical issues to deal with. They checked into Mrs. Mary Thompson's rooming house located at 325 E. 14th Street, between First and Second Avenues, once again using the aliases Mr. and Mrs. Harry Place. On June 25, 1902, Sundance purchased a watch for $15.35 at Tiffany's. Once again the happy couple moved about the city like carefree tourists, venturing to the Coney Island amusement park and visiting Sundance's brother in Atlantic City. Sundance and Etta again left New York for Buenos Aires aboard the steamer Honorius on July 10, 1902.

A peaceful retirement as prosperous South American ranchers would not be the fate of "the family of three," as Butch referred to himself and his partners in crime. The Pinkertons followed the trio's trail to Argentina, where they circulated to authorities the wanted posters featuring the famous DeYoung photograph.

By 1905, Butch, Sundance, and Etta, wanted for bank robberies in Argentina, fled to Chile and Bolivia, where their habit of committing robberies continued. Sundance and Etta traveled back to the United States in 1906, and their paths seemed to separate. While Sundance sailed back to South America to meet up with Butch, Etta apparently stayed in San Francisco, but the truth remains unknown—the mysterious Etta Place dropped out of historical sight after her return trip to the States. Historians' speculations as to what happened to Etta is all over the map. Some say

325 East 14th Street today.

she died in a shootout in Argentina. Others suggest she rode with Pancho Vila or ran a bordello in Texas.

In any event, the South American robberies continued. On November 4, 1908, along a remote trail in Bolivia, two English-speaking desperadoes encountered an express rider and relieved him of the mining-company payroll he carried.

The pair of bandits rode into the small mountain village of San Vicente and spent the night. It did not take the Bolivian authorities long to track them down. Two days later, on November 6, the duo found themselves surrounded in the small shack where they had been holed up. Gunfire ensued, and the two robbers were killed. The Bolivian soldiers later surmised that the pair were none other than the infamous Butch Cassidy and the Sundance Kid. The authorities further speculated that Butch shot Sundance before turning the gun on himself.

This speculation led to rumors that Butch and Sundance were still alive. In fact, the fate of the wanted men, and of Etta Place as well, remained unclear even to the Pinkertons. Initially they reported that "Cassidy, Longbaugh, and his 'lady friend'" were killed by the Bolivian police, but not before gunning down "more than a score of Bolivian troopers." The Pinkertons, however, continued to look for the bandits into the next decade, concluding in 1921 that the Sundance Kid was in a Peruvian jail, while Butch was still at large.

Throughout the coming years, there would be various Butch and Sundance sightings, including a claim made by Cassidy's younger sister. She claimed she met with Butch in 1925 and that he lived until 1937. In 1991, researchers dug up two graves in the old San Vicente cemetery and sent the remains for DNA analysis. The results revealed that the DNA did not match that of the outlaws' descendants. The researchers, however, rather than interpreting these finding as proof that Butch and Sundance had escaped authorities, concluded instead that they simply dug up the wrong graves. To this day, the fugitives' remains have never been positively identified, and the circumstances surrounding

Pinkerton Wanted poster (Courtesy of Utah State Historical Society).

their demise remains one of the most compelling mysteries of the Old West.

Whatever really happened to Butch, Sundance, and Etta, in all likelihood, will never be truly known. What is known for certain, however, is that in the late winter of 1901, the "family of three" were happy-go-lucky tourists in the Big Apple, living what may have been the happiest time of their lives.

The gunfighter in his New York years (Courtesy of Library of Congress LC-B21329-11).

BAT MASTERSON

"I am a Broadway guy."
WILLIAM BARCLAY "BAT" MASTERSON, 1901

On the afternoon of June 6, 1902, Bat Masterson, the 49-year-old renowned Western gunfighter and lawman, sat eating an orange on the corner of 69th Street and Columbus Avenue. Always a dandy—he had earned a reputation for dressing nattily, his head topped by an expensive derby—Masterson was having his shoes shined when he was approached by two New York City Police Detectives. The next thing Masterson knew, he was arrested and inexplicably accused of running a crooked faro game. Upon his booking, the police removed "a large pistol" from the Western gunslinger's hip pocket, and he was further charged with carrying a concealed weapon. The New York papers had a field day recounting the tale of the arrest of the famed Western shootist. The Sundance Kid and Etta Place, having recently cavorted around the city unnoticed by New York's finest, surely must have chuckled upon reading the news.

Bat was in New York to catch a ship to England, where he was scheduled to promote boxing matches set to coincide with the coronation of the new King Edward VII. The convoluted gambling charge was ultimately dropped, but Bat paid a $10 fine for the concealed weapon charge. He was most "sore" over the police failing to return his weapon. On top of everything else, Masterson also missed his ship. However, despite the auspicious start, he became enamored with New York City.

Bertholomiew Masterson was born in Quebec, Canada on November 26, 1853. The Masterson family moved to Illinois and then westward to Kansas. As a young adult, Bat, for some unexplained reason, adopted the moniker "William Barclay Masterson," which he used for the rest of his life. How Masterson became known as "Bat" is a matter of speculation. Some say he acquired the nickname when he used a walking stick or a cane—which he would use to "bat" rowdy cowboys while recovering from a gunshot wound. The most likely explanation, however, is that "Bat" was simply short for Bartholomew.

In any event, by the time Bat had turned 16, he had embarked on a violent and tumultuous life as a buffalo hunter, teamster, Army scout, lawman, and professional gambler. He counted among his friends some of the most legendary personalities of the Old West, including Doc Holliday and Wyatt Earp, the latter remaining one of Bat's lifelong friends.

The iconic legend of Bat Masterson began in the summer of 1881 when an Eastern news correspondent was in the billiard room of the Tabor House Hotel in Gunnison, Colorado, looking for stories of Western adventures. An old frontier doctor pointed out Bat Masterson and told the eager newspaperman that Masterson had killed 26 men, despite being only 27 years old. The practical-joke-playing sawbones continued spinning outlandish tales about the heroic Masterson, most of which ultimately found their way onto the pages of Eastern newspapers. Bat later disputed that he was even in Gunnison at the time, but it did not matter; the myth of Bat Masterson as the deadly gunfighter had begun. It would continue for the remainder of Bat's life, and beyond.

Even before this myth-making began, Bat had begun to earn his reputation as a man of grit as early as June 1874, when he and two dozen other buffalo hunters, trapped in a Texas-panhandle trading post, held off hundreds of Cheyenne, Comanche, and Kiowa warriors in the battle known as Adobe Walls. His legend grew in 1876, when, in Sweetwater, Texas, he got into a scrape with an Army Corporal over a saloon girl. While the fracas left Masterson wounded, the soldier and the unfortunate girl were killed in the melee.

Recovered from his wounds, Bat went on to be a deputy sheriff in the wild cow-town of Dodge City, Kansas. In 1878, he was elected Sheriff of Ford County, Kansas, where he teamed up with Wyatt Earp and gained a reputation as a tough, no-nonsense lawman. Later that year, Bat's brother Ed, a Dodge City marshal, was gunned down in front of the Lady Gay Saloon. Bat arrived at the scene too late to save his brother, but not too late to dispatch the killer.

Bat eventually wore out his welcome in Dodge City. Some thought he used his guns too quickly and spent the town's money a little too freely—he once charged Ford County $4,000 for five month's care and feeding of seven prisoners. A lawman too, his brother Jim remained in Dodge, and Bat would return now and then when his brother needed help. In 1881, he ventured to booming Tombstone, Arizona, where he was reunited with Wyatt Earp, serving on posses whenever he could tear himself away from the gaming tables.

While in Tombstone, Bat received a telegram urging him back to Dodge to assist Jim's efforts. Bat made the 1,000 mile trek and got into a gunfight as soon as he stepped off the train. The gunfight left one person injured, though Bat and Jim both went unscathed. Bat paid a $10 fine for discharging his weapon in public and left Dodge City the next morning. Masterson then became the city marshal of Trinidad, Colorado, but, in 1882, the dog-loyal Masterson would travel to Dodge City again, with Wyatt Earp at his side, when friend Sheriff Luke Short needed assistance in the atypically bloodless Wild West conflict known as the Dodge City War.

By the late 1880s, Bat had settled in Denver, Colorado, where he operated Theaters and dance halls, gambled, managed prizefighters, and promoted boxing matches. At the time, boxing had been gaining public interest, thanks in part to the popularity of heavyweight John L. Sullivan. Along the way, Bat swept off her feet a pretty young actress named Emma. Though she was a married woman, Bat was characteristically undaunted by the complication. Bat and Emma would marry in 1893 and remain together for the rest of Bat's life.

The couple traveled extensively throughout the country, with Bat refereeing and promoting fights. He also began writing a sports column for a Denver newspaper, spouting opinions and insights on boxing. By 1902, Bat had found his next career and, despite an auspicious beginning, a new home for the rest of his life: The Big Apple.

Longacre Square

In 1902, Emma and Bat moved into the Delevan Hotel on the corner of West 40th Street and Broadway. In 1904, The New York Times moved to the intersection of Broadway, Seventh Avenue, and 42nd Street, and Longacre Square would henceforth be known as Times Square. The extension of

Times Square looking South, circa 1904 (Courtesy of the Museum of the City of New York).

Times Square looking South, circa 2014.

the New York City subway system, as well as 42nd Street and Seventh Avenue becoming an express stop, cemented into the next century and beyond Times Square's future as the Crossroads of the World.

After four years at the Delevan, the couple moved into an apartment at 243 W. 43rd Street, between Seventh and Eighth Avenues. In 1910, they moved two doors up to a larger apartment at 257 W. 43rd Street, where they lived for eight years. Today, those buildings having been long ago replaced, a parking garage sits along that same stretch of West 43rd. The cost to park a car there for 24 hours is more than the $63 a month Bat used to pay for an entire month's rent in 1918.

In 1918, the couple moved into the Elmsford Apartment Building, located at 300 W. 49th Street, at the corner of Eighth Avenue. The six-story building still exists today as the Elmsford Apartments.

The Elmsford Apartments today.

The Morning Telegraph

In 1903, Bat joined the staff of the Morning Telegraph as a sportswriter, focusing on, but certainly not limiting himself to, boxing. The Morning telegraph sought a sophisticated clientele and specialized in sporting and entertainment news. For decades the editors bragged that it was the most expensive newspaper in the United States. By 1920, the selling price of the Sunday edition had risen to an unheard of 10 cents. One of the paper's writers has been credited with coining the term the "Big Apple" when referring to New York's horse-racing industry in 1920. The offices of the Morning Telegraph were located at 525 W. 52nd Street, between 10th and 11th Avenues, a short walk from Bat's last residence at the corner of Eighth Avenue and 49th Street. The building still stands today.

For the next 18 years, Masterson would write three times a week a lengthy column that came to be titled "Masterson's Views on Timely Topics." Although some of the columns were, frankly, almost unreadable, Bat had a unique no-holds-barred writing style. He often would sprinkle his articles with colorful but somewhat confusing observations, such as calling the unfortunate loser of a boxing match "a fine piece of cheese." Here are just a couple of other examples:

> "There are more ways to kill a dog than by choking him to death with a piece of custard pie."
> "Every dog, we are told, has his day, unless there are more dogs than days."

Masterson fan Damon Runyon, who would base on Bat the Guys and Dolls character Sky Masterson, probably critiqued Bat's writing ability best when he surmised, "Bat had no literary style, but he had plenty of moxie."

Courthouse Battles

Although Bat's Western gun-fighting days were well behind him by the time he turned to journalism, he had lost none of his feistiness. His column routinely fired salvos at politicians, boxers, and fight promoters. Any perceived slight aimed at Masterson also was likely to be answered by a lawsuit. One time, Bat sued for libel a New York City newspaper that had printed that Masterson "made his reputation by shooting drunken Mexicans and Indians in the back." The case set the stage for a dramatic cross-examination of Masterson by future United States Supreme Court Justice Benjamin N. Cardozo. On May 20, 1913, in the old Tweed Courthouse, located at 52 Chambers Street, Cardozo, a legend in his own right in legal circles, aggressively questioned the 59-year-old gunfighter about his Western exploits. His first question: "How many men have you shot and killed in your life?" Bat denied the persistent story that he had killed 28 men and finally admitted the number slain to be "about three." When pressed by Cardozo, Masterson admitted that he also shot a man in Dodge City in 1881, but wasn't sure if he killed him or not. When asked if he had killed any Indians, Bat responded that he wasn't sure, but added that "I certainly did try to shoot them … it wasn't my fault that I didn't hit them. … I haven't any idea of and can't give you any notion as to whether any of them fell under my fire." Masterson won the libel suit and was awarded $3,500, a sum reduced to $1,000 on appeal.

The old Tweed Courthouse located behind City Hall on Chambers Street.

The Old Tweed Courthouse is located on the north side of City Hall Park, behind City Hall, on Chambers Street between Centre Street and Broadway (above). Its construction spanned 20 years, from 1861 to 1881, and was awash in corruption. The project was overseen by the watchful eye and outstretched palm of William M. "Boss" Tweed, the Tammany Hall Boss who ran New York politics for decades. Ironically, Boss Tweed was tried and convicted in an unfinished courtroom in his Courthouse in 1873. The three-and-half-story stone structure underwent a major restoration in 1999. Today, it houses the headquarters of the New York City Department of Education.

A SPORTING MAN

Bat Masterson seems to have made an effortless transition from Western gunslinger to Broadway sporting man. He meshed well with the New York newspapermen, who were understandably in awe of the Western lawman. It was a man's world in 1900, and Bat was a man's man. By the turn of the century, theaters and restaurants were moving up to Broadway, from lower Manhattan to Longacre Square, and Bat was happy to be in the middle of the action.

One of Bat's favorite hangouts was Shanley's Restaurant, located at 207 W. 43rd Street. In 1910, Shanley's moved across Broadway to a more spacious location in the Longacre Building, which extended along Broadway from 43rd to 44th Street. Shanley's was a popular watering hall for New York's sporting men, who were attracted by the bustling atmosphere and 75-cent lunches. The Shanley Restaurants would not survive prohibition. Most of Bat's old haunts in Times Square, including the Longacre Building, did not escape the wrecking ball that came with the rejuvenation and Disneyfication of Times Square in the early 1990s.

Bat was a regular at the bar of the Metropole Hotel, where he would enjoy a Tom Collins cocktail. The Metropole Hotel was located in a narrow six-story building on the north side of 43rd Street, about 50 yards from Broadway. It was the first hotel in New York City to have running water, and on July 16, 1912 was the scene of the murder of notorious

Michael P. O'Connor

Hotel Metropole, 1900 (Courtesy of the Museum of the City of New York).

New York gambler Herman Rosenthal. Bat claimed he saw bullet holes in the façade of the hotel. Fortunately, the building has survived and, today, is the location of the Casablanca Hotel, which accurately boasts that it is just steps away from Times Square.

Bat also enjoyed the café at the luxurious Waldorf-Astoria Hotel, on Fifth Avenue and 34th Street. The opulent hotel had a staff of 1,500 people who catered to New York's fashionable society. On the night of June 22, 1906, in the café, the aging gunfighter made short work of an old Colorado acquaintance who had held a grudge against Masterson and had been badmouthing him around the New York saloons. Bat laid out the larger man with one well-placed punch, and was reportedly observed flashing a revolver. Masterson shrugged off the incident as an insignificant dust-up, and claimed the revolver was actually a pack of cigarettes. The old Waldorf–Astoria was razed in 1929 to make way for the Empire State Building.

As a well-known man-about-town, Bat was a sought-after guest and was occasionally persuaded to attend fraternal dinners. In December 1913, he participated in a Friars' Club roast of David Warfield. The event took place in the ninth-floor ballroom of the Hotel Astor, a popular Times Square venue. The 11-story hotel, built in 1904, took

The original Metropole Hotel Building on 42nd Street.

73

up a full city block along Broadway, between West 44th and West 45th Streets. The era of the Hotel Astor ended with its closing in 1967. The building was razed in the late 1960s, and the site is now occupied by the 54-story One Astor Plaza.

United States Marshal Bat Masterson
President Teddy Roosevelt, an aficionado of the Wild West, was into his second term when, in February 1905, he appointed William Barclay Masterson as a Deputy United States Marshal for the Southern District of New York, a job that paid an annual salary of $2,000. Although Roosevelt had been born in a brownstone off Park Avenue, silver spoon planted firmly in his mouth, he considered himself a Westerner at heart and relished associating with Western legends like Buffalo Bill Cody and, of course, the legendary Bat Masterson. Roosevelt, not above giving political appointments to his Western heroes, had previously appointed the killer of Billy the Kid, lawman Pat Garrett, as the collector of customs in El Paso, Texas. Roosevelt was not oblivious to the criticism that would be raised by another similarly inspired appointment, and cautioned Bat that he "must be careful not to gamble or do anything while […] a public officer which might afford opportunity to [Bat's] enemies and [Roosevelt's] critics to say [Bat's] appointment was improper."

Bat took his oath of office in the old City Hall Post Office, where the Marshal's offices were located. The French Renaissance-style building was built in 1880 for the at-the-time mind-boggling cost of $8.5 million. It was situated at the tip of City Hall Park, facing down Broadway, across from the Woolworth Building. The building, which from the beginning was criticized for its architectural design ("a showy granite building") and proximate location to City Hall Park, was declared obsolete by 1921 and finally torn down as part of the city's beautification effort for the 1939 World's Fair. It appears that Masterson's duties consisted mainly of picking up his paycheck, since he maintained his position at the Morning Telegraph. When William Howard Taft assumed the Presidency in 1909, Masterson's tenure as a Deputy U.S. Marshal came to an end.

525 West 52nd Street today, site of Bat Masterson's death.

William Barclay "Bat" Masterson was not destined to perish under a hail of gunfire on a dusty street in a lawless Western cowtown. Rather, his demise was likely the result of too many $3 steaks at Shanley's. On October 25, 1921, the 68-year-old adventurer turned sportswriter suffered a massive heart attack and was found slumped over his typewriter at the Morning Telegraph offices. He had just finished what would be his last column. Still in the typewriter was Bat's final cynical observation: "There are those who argue that everything breaks even in this old dump of a world of ours. I suppose these ginks who argue that way hold that because the rich man gets ice in the summer and the poor man gets it in the winter things are breaking even for both. Maybe so, but I'll swear I can't see it that way …"

Funeral services were held at Campbell's Funeral Parlor at Broadway and 66th Street, and Masterson is buried in Woodlawn Cemetery in the Bronx. Over the next century, Campbell's would develop a niche for providing discrete funeral services for rich and famous cadavers like Rudolph Valentino, Jacqueline Kennedy Onassis, James Cagney, Greta Garbo, Mae West, Joan Crawford, John Lennon, and Ed Sullivan. Campbell's Funeral Home moved to 81st and Madison in 1938.

The death of Bat Masterson made national news and prompted the press to revive all of Bat's exaggerated exploits, including his supposed slaying of 26 men during his Wild West years. *The New York Times* lamented that Bat was "the last of the old time gun fighters" (although Wyatt Earp was alive and well and unsuccessfully attempting to peddle his story to the infant film industry in California).

The name "Bat Masterson" would forever conjure in American culture images of a Western lawman and gunfighter, not of a New York newspaperman. Over the coming decades, the Bat Masterson character would pop up in movies and television shows, usually as the dapper sidekick of Wyatt Earp. In 1958, Gene Barry played the title role in the television series *Bat Masterson*. For four seasons, Barry played Bat as a meticulously dressed cane-carrying gambler and adventurer, subduing evildoers and lovely ladies throughout the West.

Ignoring the fact that he was Canadian, which he himself did, William Barclay Masterson led a uniquely American life. He hunted buffalo and fought Indians when the West was still wild, yet lived long enough to see Babe Ruth play baseball. He dined with President Theodore Roosevelt and stood shoulder to shoulder with Wyatt Earp in Tombstone and Dodge City, and was, for the last two decades of his life, a revered and respected fixture in the nightlife and sporting world of New York City.

Buffalo Bill Cody c. 1911 (Courtesy of Library of Congress LC-USZ62-2050).

BUFFALO BILL CODY

> *"I had been in New York about 20 days when General Sheridan arrived in the city. In answer to a question how I was enjoying myself, I replied that I had struck the best camp I had ever seen ..."*
> BUFFALO BILL CODY, 1872

In 1872, the 26-year-old William Frederick Cody, on leave from his Army scouting duties, found himself called from the audience to take a bow on the stage of New York's Bowery Theater. In the same theater where the Honorable David Crockett had sat over three decades earlier, Cody found himself the center of attention and spoke a few "utterances that were inaudible even to the leader of the orchestra." The real-life Buffalo Bill was attending the opening night of a theatrical drama entitled *Buffalo Bill, the King of the Border Men*, which was loosely (emphasis on loosely) based on the exploits of Buffalo Bill Cody.

Thanks in large measure to the vast popularity of dime novels, by the time he took the stage that night in the Bowery, William Frederick Cody was known throughout the country as "Buffalo Bill." The mass-produced, inexpensive paperbacks thrilled both Westerners and Eastern dudes eager to read of frontier exploits and fearless heroes. Since 1869, Cody had been a popular subject thanks to writer

Edward Judson, who used the pseudonym "Ned Buntline." Buntline, a New Yorker, was a colorful character in his own right. In 1846, he was tried for murder in Tennessee for killing his girlfriend's husband in a duel, and although he was acquitted, he was shot and wounded during the course of the trial and barely escaped a lynch mob. Buntline, clearly owning an eye for the ladies, would ultimately marry six times.

Buntline traveled back to New York City, where he didn't fare much better than he had Tennessee. He spent a year in jail for being one of the instigators of the 1849 Astor Place Riot that left 23 New Yorkers dead. He served with the Union Army during the Civil War, but was discharged for drunkenness. He also owns his own unique place in Western lore. The legend goes that in 1876, Buntline presented custommade Colt Revolvers to five Dodge City lawmen, including Wyatt Earp and Bat Masterson. The pistols had oversized 16-inch barrels with "Ned" carved into the walnut handles. Wyatt Earp's biographer, Stuart Lake, claimed it was Wyatt's favorite gun. Western historians and enthusiasts have been arguing about and searching in vain for the elusive "Buntline Special" revolver ever since.

Whatever else Buntline may have been, there is little doubt he was a prolific and financially successful writer churning hundreds of stories for various publications. He had come across Cody in 1867 while Cody was hunting Buffalo for the Kansas Pacific Railroad. By the time the two met, Cody had already earned the monicker "Buffalo Bill" for killing over 4,000 bison in an 18-month period. Buntline began writing of the heroic adventures of "Buffalo Bill," which became wildly popular.

Although Buntline clearly exaggerated Cody's exploits, the same as subsequent authors who would ultimately churn out more than 500 dime novels featuring Buffalo Bill, Cody was, to a great extent, the real deal. At the age of 14, he rode for the Pony Express, and in 1863, at the tender age of 16, he joined the Union Army as a teamster for the Seventh Kansas Cavalry. He later claimed the enlistment resulted from "a night of bad whiskey." From 1868 until 1872, he was an Army scout, where his fearless demeanor and formidable frontier skills culminated in a Congressional Medal of Honor for gallantry in action as a civilian scout.

In 1872, the Army utilized Cody's fame by enlisting him as a guide for influential foreign royalty anxious to hunt in the Wild West. Cody entertained dignitaries like Russia's Grand Duke Alexis, who was thoroughly impressed with his flamboyant guide. The lavish excursion, which included General Phillip Sheridan and Brevet General George Armstrong Custer, himself no shrinking violet, was a promotional success.

More importantly, Cody learned the value of showmanship. In addition to his larger-than-life personality, he was also a sight to behold. His long hair flowed from beneath a white sombrero. He wore buckskins over a crimson shirt and was mounted on a beautiful white horse. His fame was spreading, and he knew it.

A RELUCTANT ACTOR

Buffalo Bill's rising star, and his seemingly unlimited potential, was not lost on the ambitious and prolific Buntline. In the winter of 1872, he hastily wrote a play tailor made for Buffalo Bill, *The Scouts of the Prairie*. With a little prodding,

Edward Zane Carrol Judson (Buntline), Buffalo Bill and Jack Omohundro (Courtesy of Library of Congress USZ62-51647).

Cody was convinced to star in the show, which opened in Chicago in December 1872. Joining him on stage were Texas Jack Omohundro, a fellow scout, and, of course, Ned Buntline. By all accounts, the play was ridiculous, but crowds were fascinated by the spectacle of seeing the real Buffalo Bill kill off hordes of Indians with blank cartridges.

The Scouts of the Prairie opened in New York City at the Niblo's Garden Theater on April 1, 1873, to somewhat tepid reviews. The *New York Herald* declared "everything was so wonderfully bad it was almost good." But it did not matter; New York audiences loved it. The sometimes-sober trio were joined on stage by an Italian ballerina playing an Indian maiden and a menagerie of whatever unfortunate locals could be rounded up and covered in war paint to play "Pawnee chiefs." The absurdity of the melodrama peaked in the second act when Buntline, a notorious drinker, delivered a temperance lecture. *The New York Times* kindly noted that the lecture "was calculated to do much good."

Niblo's Garden was a popular theater located in downtown Manhattan at the corner of Broadway and Prince Street, extending to Crosby Street on the east and Houston Street on the west. Niblo's Garden started in 1823 as an open-air coffee shop also serving ice cream and lemonade. Through the years, it evolved into a premiere "pleasure garden" with an open-air saloon and a first-class theater that held over 3,000 patrons. During his 1872 visit, Buffalo Bill enjoyed passing his evenings at Niblo's and watching the long-running musical comedy *The Black Crook*. Niblo's Garden closed its doors in 1895 and was quickly demolished, making way for a 12-story commercial building.

While in New York City for the run of *The Scouts of the Prairie*, Buffalo Bill stayed at the Brevoort Place Hotel and the Union Club.

Built in 1845 in the heart of Greenwich Village, and stretching along Fifth Avenue between East 8th and 9th Streets, the large Brevoort Hotel was considered one of the finest in New York. By the early 1900s, it would have a French fair and would be a favorite gathering spot for New York's literary crowd, including Mark Twain and Eugene

Niblo's Hotel, 1851 (Courtesy of New York Public Library).

Broadway and Prince Street today.

85

O'Neill. In 1933, aviator Charles Lindbergh collected the $25,000 prize for his transatlantic flight at the Brevoort.

The hotel was demolished in 1954 to make way for an apartment complex. Today, it is the site of the 20-story

Brevoort Hotel c. 1904 (Courtesy of the Museum of the City of New York).

Brevoort Apartment complex today.

Brevoort Co-op Apartment complex at 11 Fifth Avenue. The complex occupies a full city block bounded by Fifth Avenue, East 8th Street, University Place, and East 9th Street. Apartments there sell for well over $1 million.

The Union Club is a prestigious and exclusive private social club that dates back to 1836. The Union Club remains, as it did during its heyday, extremely conservative; women were not allowed even to be seen in the members' areas until 1918, when the shortage of male employees caused by World War I forced the club to hire women as waitresses. Through the decades, its list of impressive members has included John Jacob Astor, Ulysses S. Grant, Philip Sheridan, William Tecumseh Sherman, William Randolph Hearst, and Cornelius Vanderbilt. In 1872, when Buffalo Bill strode its grounds, the Union Club was located in a mansion at the northwest corner of Fifth Avenue and 21st Street. In 1903, the old mansion was demolished to make way for an 11-story commercial building that still stands today. Currently, the Union Club is located at the northeast corner of 69th Street and Park Avenue and is still considered one of the most exclusive private clubs in the country.

AN ADDITION TO THE TROUPE

In the late-summer of 1873, Buffalo Bill convinced an old friend and fellow scout to join him in New York City for a run in a new production. In the 1873–1874 theatrical season, *The Scouts of the Plains* would play at the Bowery Theater, at Wood's Museum on Broadway and 30th Street, and over in Brooklyn at both the Olympic Theater and the Brooklyn Academy of Music. Buffalo Bill had cautioned his "pard" to be mindful of the New York hack drivers, since they were likely to cheat unsuspecting passengers. It turned out to be sage advice. Upon arriving in the city, Buffalo Bill's guest, well-informed and meticulously dressed, refused to pay one such hack driver's inflated fare. The driver cursed out the stylish Westerner, who handled the situation as only a son of the Wild West could: he left the hack driver sprawled out on Fifth Avenue and calmly walked into the Brevoort Hotel. Wild Bill Hickok had taken his first bite of the Big Apple, and The *Kansas City Examiner* happily reported that Wild Bill was "airing his long hair" in New York City.

James Butler Hickok was born in 1837 in Illinois. At age 18, he drifted to Leavenworth, Kansas, which was embroiled in sectional rivalry and violence leading up to the Civil War. A staunch pro-Union man, Hickok was in the thick of the unparalleled bloodshed. Prior to the Civil War, Hickok also worked as a Pony Express rider, teamster, and buffalo hunter, where he met his lifelong friend, Buffalo Bill Cody. Hickok's notoriety started to spread when he shot two men in Rock Creek, Nebraska, in a dispute over a woman, which would be a recurring theme in Wild Bill's short but eventful life.

At the outbreak of the Civil War, Hickok joined the Union Army and became one of George Armstrong Custer's scouts. In 1865, Wild Bill participated in a classic gunfight in the Springfield, Missouri public square. Despite Hollywood's version of the gunfight, which typically pitted good guy against bad, each facing the other on a dusty western street, gunfights rarely, if ever, happened that way. However, on July 21, 1869, the tall, muscular Wild Bill Hickok, with his long hair and flowing mustache, stepped into the street, two revolvers shoved in his belt, to meet his antagonist, Dave Tutt. Bad blood flowed between the two because of a gambling debt and, of course, a woman. The two gunfighters stood 70 yards apart and fired almost simultaneously. When the smoke cleared, Tutt was dead, and a Western legend was born. Hickok later wore a badge in the wild and wooly cow towns of Hays City and Abilene.

Like Buffalo Bill, Hickok saw his legend spread thanks to dime novels and self-promotion. However, unlike his friend, Wild Bill was unable, and perhaps unwilling, to make the transition from Western frontier to Eastern society. What you saw was what you got. On stage, he was an unmitigated disaster. When he couldn't remember his lines, which was most of the time, he simply ad-libbed and told jokes. He would break the floodlights if they bothered his eyes, so you can imagine what hecklers were in for if they were unfortunate enough to steal Wild Bill's attention. He demanded real whiskey instead of cold tea for his drinking scenes, and he would not leave the show's "Indian maidens" alone. He had a particularly annoying habit of shooting the blank cartridges close to the "Pawnee chiefs," burning the unfortunate actors. Off stage, he behaved even worse. He was given to marathon drunks and did not suffer fools gladly. On one particular night, he ran into a problem with five or six men in a lower Manhattan poolroom. The men were making sport at Hickok's long hair and fancy dress. The incident did not end well for the New Yorkers, and when the concerned Cody asked Wild Bill where he had been, he coolly responded, "I got lost among the hostiles."

SAY CHEESE
While in New York, the dashing Hickok, who loved to have his photograph taken, took full advantage of the photogra-

GURNEY & SON,   FIFTH AVE, N. Y.

Wild Bill Hickok c. 1873.

phy studios on Broadway. By the middle of the nineteenth century, innovations in photography had made portraits extremely popular, and the most accomplished photographers in the nation had studios along lower Broadway. Jeremiah Gurney had a studio at 707 Broadway; Napoleon Sarony had a studio at 680 Broadway; and the famous Civil War photographer Matthew Brady had a studio at 785 Broadway. By the time of Hickok's visit in 1873, Brady was immersed in a messy bankruptcy, and the photographic treasures in his New York Studio were being seized to satisfy debts.

Hickok chose another photographer, George Rockwood, to capture his image. He sat for a group shot with Buffalo Bill and Texas Jack, as well as a separate portrait, at

Rockwood's studio, located at 839 Broadway, at the corner of 13th Street. The business would be a coupe for Rockwood, as there was fierce competition among the photographers for the lucrative celebrity-photograph business. The images that were taken of the rich and famous were turned into carte de visites, which were calling-card-sized photographic images that could be reproduced and sold. Since the introduction of the daguerreotype in the 1840s, photography studios had been leapfrogging one another up Broadway.

Brady Studio, 359 Broadway between Franklin and Leonard Streets.

The studios would continue to migrate uptown to Union Square. By 1873, Sarony had moved to 37 Union Square, where Hickok would sit for another portrait. By the end of the 1870s, Rockwood would also move to 17 Union Square. Sadly, the only building that has survived from this golden age of photography is the building Mathew Brady used as a studio from 1853 to 1860, at 359 Broadway, between Franklin and Leonard Streets.

EXIT STAGE RIGHT

Wild Bill continued to tour through the East in early 1874 with the merry band, which by then had begun calling itself "Buffalo Bill's Combination Troupe," but his behavior, on and off the stage, only worsened. The drinking and brawls continued, and finally Hickok left the troupe after the second act of *The Scouts of the Plains* in Rochester, New York, much to everyone's relief, especially the "Pawnee chiefs," who were growing weary of getting singed by Wild Bill's carelessly placed blanks. Despite the tumultuous experience, the two friends parted on good terms, with Cody giving Hickok $1,000 for his trouble. On his way back to the West, however, Wild Bill made a final stop in New York City, where he promptly lost the money in a faro game.

Wild Bill returned to his element in Cheyenne, Wyoming, but he was not the man he had been a decade before. Historians speculate that Hickok was never the same after he accidentally killed his deputy marshal during a gunfight in Abilene in 1871. In any event, with his eyesight failing, the newly married Wild Bill, a man much older than his 39 years suggested, rolled into the boomtown of Deadwood, South Dakota, eager to make his fortune.

On August 2, 1876, James Butler Hickok was gambling in Saloon No. 10 when a drifter named Jack McCall walked behind him and put a bullet in the back of his head. The mortally wounded Hickok was clutching pairs of aces and eights, henceforth known in poker parlance as the "Dead Man's Hand."

FIRST SCALP FOR CUSTER
After Hickok bid his fellow thespians adieu in the early winter of 1874, the show continued on from Rochester without him. Buffalo Bill would sometimes inject Kit Carson Jr., the son of the famous scout, into the cast for added star power.

By 1876, Cody had settled into a routine of touring with his combination troupe from the fall until the early spring, and then depart for the solitude of the West to do some hunting.

1876 would also prove to be an eventful, albeit somewhat tragic, year for Buffalo Bill Cody. On April 21, 1876, his pride and joy, his 5-year-old son, Kit Carson Cody, passed away from scarlet fever in Rochester. Cody never recovered from this devastating loss, and he returned to the stage with a heavy heart.

In early July 1876, the United States was jolted from its centennial celebration by the news that, on June 25, the seemingly invincible Indian fighter, George Armstrong Custer, and his entire command had been wiped out by an overwhelming number of Lakota and Cheyenne warriors by the Little Bighorn River in Montana.

Custer's old scout sprang into action. Cody had already closed the theatrical season early and was scouting for the Army in Wyoming Territory when he received the news about Custer and the 7th Cavalry. On July 17, 1876, just weeks after the battle that ended Custer, Cody found himself with the Fifth U.S. Cavalry in a skirmish with Cheyenne warriors on a desolate plain near Warbonnet Creek in Northwestern Nebraska. Cody, determined to avenge his friend's death, shot and killed a young warrior named Yellow Hair, and, to the shouts and cheers of the troopers, proceeded to scalp him. Cody, dressed in buckskins and his crimson shirt, raised the grisly trophy and dramatically stated that he had just taken the first scalp for Custer.

For reasons no one but Cody could possibly know, he boxed up Yellow Hair's bloody scalp and shipped it to his wife, Lulu, who immediately fainted upon opening the package she foolishly thought was a gift.

BUFFALO BILL'S WILD WEST

For the next seven years, Cody continued his theatrical performances, which included a highly successful reenactment of the scalping of Yellow Hair, but the old buffalo hunter had more ambitious plans. In 1882, Cody organized and performed an outdoor show that included real Indians and real cowboys. Cody would continue *The Wild West Show*, in one form or another, for the next 30 years. The climax of the performance would be a reenactment of Custer's last stand, with Buffalo Bill riding a white charger, arriving "too late" to rescue his friend.

The Wild West Show would tour all over North America and Europe, but Buffalo Bill had a soft spot for New York City. Buffalo Bill's Wild West would make more than 15 appearances in New York City over the years and would play separate engagements in Staten Island and Brooklyn.

Parades up Broadway would mark *The Wild West's* arrival in New York, with the buckskin-clad Buffalo Bill on his white charger, leading his cast, which sometimes stood 500 strong.

Sitting Bull

In the aftermath of the Battle of the Little Bighorn, the chief of the Lakotas, Sitting Bull, emerged as the Native American most closely associated with Custer's Last Stand. Newspaper accounts depicted Sitting Bull as the shrewd architect of the battle plan, with some accounts even crediting Sitting Bull with the killing of Custer. In truth, the victory over the 7th Cavalry was due more to the folly of the reckless Custer than the military genius of the Lakota Chief. Sitting Bull's active role in the battle was limited. He acted more as an influential shaman or medicine man than a direct combatant. Nevertheless, the now-famous Sitting Bull could not be allowed by the United States to roam free. After five years of evading the relentless pursuit of the Army, and even fleeing to Canada at one point, on July 19, 1881, the 50-year-old Sitting Bull and his followers reluctantly surrendered to federal authorities in Dakota Territory.

Sitting Bull was ultimately sent to the Standing Rock Reservation in Dakota Territory, and in 1884 received government permission to leave the reservation to participate in a theatrical production touted as *The Sitting Bull Combination*, which advertised Sitting Bull as "the slayer of General Custer." The show toured 25 cities, and included a two-week engagement in September at the Eden Musée, which was located at 55 W. 23rd Street, near Sixth Avenue. The arrival of Sitting Bull and his companions in New York created quite a stir among New Yorkers eager to catch a

Buffalo Bill and Sitting Bull c. 1885 (Courtesy of Library of Congress LC-USZ62-21202).

glimpse of the famous Lakota Chief. The press noted that Sitting Bull "looked much stouter than when he surrendered at Fort Buford," and that he was attired in "a shirt of marvelous uncleanliness, and a wide-brimmed felt hat … Mrs. Bull was dressed in green and her hair was tied with red leather, and she carried a sharp knife in her left hand."

Sitting Bull settled comfortably in the Grand Central Hotel, where he was immediately given a bath. He especially relished the dining room, where he would eat three beefsteaks at a sitting, followed by several portions of ice cream. He commented that such a hotel should be built at the Standing Rock Reservation.

The Grand Central Hotel was located at 673 Broadway at West 31st Street. It opened in 1870 on the site of the Winter Garden Theatre, which was destroyed by fire in 1867. At the time, the Grand Central Hotel was the largest hotel ever constructed in the United States, boasting 650 rooms spread out over eight floors. For decades the hotel hosted New York's elite, but by the 1960s it had fallen on hard times and was turned into a welfare hotel. In 1973, the hotel, then named the Broadway Central Hotel, collapsed, killing four residents. The building was razed, and today the site is home to New York University dorms.

Cody, the ultimate showman, saw Sitting Bull's enormous box office potential and received government permission to employ him for the 1885 theatrical season. Sitting Bull signed on in June 1885 for $125 and was paid $50 a week. He would make extra cash by selling his autograph for a dollar. The playbills proclaimed: "Foes in '76, Friends in '85." While working with Cody on the production, Sitting Bull became so enthralled with another star performer, sharpshooter Annie Oakley, that he wanted to adopt her. The show played New York City in the summer of 1885 and was a great success. While performing, Sitting

Grand Central Hotel c. 1880 (Courtesy of the Museum of the City of New York).

Site of Grand Central Hotel today at 673 Broadway between 34th Street and West 3rd. Note the imprint of the former 8 story hotel on the neighboring building.

Bull wore buckskin, war paint, and a feathered headdress, but he walked the streets of New York City in a brocade waistcoat, black flowered pants, a scarlet tie, printed shirt, and rubber-soled moccasins.

Sitting Bull only lasted four months on stage. The hard feelings between Sitting Bull and the rest of the nation over the killing of Custer had not fully subsided, especially in the West, and many resented that Sitting Bull seemed to be cashing in on his prominent role in the massacre. Buffalo Bill was unable to secure permission for Sitting Bull's return, and Sitting Bull was anxious to escape the constant crowds and to return to Standing Rock and his beloved Dakota Territory. Before he left, the disappointed Cody presented Sitting Bull with a trick horse and a Stetson hat in appreciation for the old warrior's services. The two men would never see each other again.

Upon his return to Standing Rock, a Western newspaper reported that "Sitting Bull and his band of dingy dudes" had arrived back, and "Sitting Bull's abdomen was as round as a barrel."

By 1890, Sitting Bull and the Indian Agents were once again at odds. The Lakota Chief was seen as a threat because of his participation in the Ghost Dance, a religious movement being blamed for trouble on Sioux reservations. Cody would travel to Standing Rock in early December 1890 to see Sitting Bull but would be denied permission. Two weeks later, on December 15, 1890, Sitting Bull was shot and killed by Indian police in a tragically botched attempt to arrest him.

Sitting Bull's murder panicked the Lakotas. They believed that the government was going to kill them all off. Lakota bands began leaving reservations in the dead of winter in a desperate attempt to reach what they hoped would be the safety of the Pine Ridge Reservation, where the influential Red Cloud had settled. On December 29,1890, Custer's old command, the 7th Cavalry, surrounded a Lakota encampment on the bank of the Wounded Knee Creek in South Dakota and attempted to disarm the Lakotas. What began as a scuffle between a soldier and a deaf tribesman who refused to surrender his rifle escalated horribly. Troopers haphazardly opened fire into the camp, mowing down mostly women and children. The result was the wholesale slaughter of over 300 Native Americans, an act known since as the Wounded Knee Massacre.

Madison Square Garden
Buffalo Bill played Madison Square Garden for the first time in 1886, and for the last time in 1913. Buffalo Bill loved playing at the Garden, partly because old comrades in arms, such as Phil Sheridan and William Tecumseh Sherman, who had relocated to New York, could watch and enjoy the elaborate performances. In 1886, *Buffalo Bill's Wild West Show* played to over a million people. After performances at the Garden, Cody also made it a ritual to hold private receptions for the graduating seniors of the United States Military Academy at West Point.

In 1886, Madison Square Garden was located on the northeast corner of Madison Square on East 26th Street. The indoor arena, which could hold 10,000 people, had been used previously as a circus arena by P.T. Barnum. By 1913, the building had been replaced by a larger 32-story structure that remained until 1925. Where those buildings once stood

Madison Square Garden, c. 1905 (Courtesy of the Museum of the City of New York).

now stands the New York Life Insurance Building, which encompasses the entire block. Since 1968, Madison Square Garden has been located between Seventh and Eighth Avenues from 31st to 33rd Streets. The location is on the site of the 1910 architectural and engineering marvel, Penn Station, which was razed in 1963.

Modern site of old Madison Square Garden.

LEGAL WOES

In the decades that followed, Cody consistently had cash flow problems. He took on various partners and investors to help cope with the daunting logistical requirements of the traveling *Wild West Show*. The overhead was enormous; hundreds of performers, cattle, horses, and buffalo, all of which had to be fed. Cash poured in, but it poured out just as quickly.

As a result of his varied business entanglements, Cody was frequently in court as both a litigant and a witness. He spent a fair amount of time in the old Tweed Courthouse on Chambers Street. On one particular occasion, in October 1894, when Buffalo Bill was being sued for breach of contract, he requested a long adjournment so he could leave New York to return to the West. The judge sternly replied, "It is wholly immaterial to me whether you want to hunt in the western country or not. This case must be tried."

Cody also ended up in court in Wyoming on a purely personal matter when he sued his wife of 38 years, Louisa (he called her Lulu) for divorce in 1904. Contemporary celebrity divorce proceeding have nothing on the infamous Cody divorce trial. Allegations flew fast and furious, and the press relished printing the sordid accusations of Cody's drinking and womanizing. Lulu went so far as to claim that Buffalo Bill had an affair with Queen Victoria, an accusation the judge promptly struck from the record but the newspapers couldn't resist publishing. In the end, the judge, sympathetic to Lulu's plight, refused to grant Cody a divorce. He found Buffalo Bill's claim that Lulu tried to poison him to be unsupported by the evidence. Rather, the judge surmised that Lulu had actually been trying to revive Cody from a state of intoxication when she spiked his drink with some unknown concoction. The judge also found that her poisoning of Buffalo Bill's favorite pet dogs had been accidental. One of the interesting tidbits that emerged from the trial and depositions was that during one of Buffalo Bill's trips to New York in the spring of 1898, Lulu sought to surprise her husband by showing up unannounced at his room at the Hoffman House. When she telephoned the room from the lobby, it was Lulu who was surprised when a female voice answered the phone. Lulu left in a rage and checked into the Waldorf Astoria, where she proceeded to smash mirrors, furniture, and vases in the lobby. The stately Waldorf Astoria simply sent Cody the bill.

The Hoffman House, early 1900s (Courtesy of Museum of the City of New York).

Broadway and 25th today. The obelisk in the foreground was erected in 1857 over the tomb of General William Jenkins Worth, a veteran of the Seminole War, and the Mexican War. Fort Worth, Texas is named after the General.

Cody often made his headquarters at the Hoffman House during his New York appearances. The Hoffman House was erected in 1864 on the corner of Broadway and 25th Street. It was famous for its luxuriously furnished bar and risqué art décor. In the late nineteenth century the Hoffman House was considered one of the main attractions of uptown night-life. By 1910, the center of New York's after-hours attractions had moved up to the Times Square area, and the Hoffman House went bankrupt, struggling along until 1915, when it finally shut its doors and was razed.

Michael P. O'Connor

PUTTIN ON THE OL' FEEDBAG

When not holding court at the elegant Hoffman House bar, Cody could be found at the Waldorf Astoria café. He did not need much convincing to participate in formal social functions either. On April 3, 1910, he attended a Friars' Club dinner honoring George M. Cohan in the ballroom of the Hotel Astor. The Hotel Astor, located on Broadway between 44th and 45th Streets, was built at the staggering cost of $7 million in 1904 and was a fixture in the theater district for over half a century. The lavishly furnished hotel housed a large ballroom that could accommodate 500 diners and a rooftop garden that was a popular venue for New Yorkers and tourists alike.

Buffalo Bill also took full advantage of New York's world-renowned steakhouses. Keens Steakhouse has been operating out of the same building at 72 W. 36th Street, in what was then the Theater District, by Herald Square, since 1885. Keens was a popular hangout with the theatrical crowd, and had evolved as part of the Lambs Club, which was a London-based private social group comprised of literary and theatrical gentleman. For $5 a year, Lambs Club members could keep their hard-clay long-stem pipes at the restaurant under the supervision of a "pipe warden." The Pipe Club now has over 90,000 names on its roster. Some of the most famous members' clay pipes are on display, including those belonging to Teddy Roosevelt, Will Rogers, Babe Ruth, and, of course, Buffalo Bill Cody. If you want to smoke your clay pipe today, however, you have to go outside, since smoking has been banned in New York City restaurants since 2003.

Keens Steakhouse today at 72 West 36th Street.

Thanks to Lily Langtry, the renowned and beautiful actress, women have been allowed inside the premises since 1905, when Langtry successfully sued the steakhouse to gain entrance.

Buffalo Bill was first introduced to the legendary Delmonico's Steakhouse in 1872, when he was somewhat surprised to find out that the $50 he had in his pocket did not cover a scrumptious meal for a party of 12. Luckily, Ned Buntline bailed him out, and Delmonico's had a steady customer for life. Delmonico's Steakhouse has been in operation in New York City, in one form or another, since 1827. During its heyday at the turn of the century, it had four locations in Manhattan. One of the Delmonico's was located on the southwest corner of Fifth Avenue and East 26th Street, conveniently located across the street from the Hoffman House.

Its flagship restaurant since 1837 was located at South William Street and Beaver Street (56 Beaver). The grand entrance to the building was supported by two massive marble pillars claimed to be imported from the ruins of Pompeii. In 1891, the space was restored into an eight-story structure that still occupies a triangle of a building at South William and Beaver Streets (page 111). For decades, Delmonico's would serve host to the city's most famous residents and guests, including Abraham Lincoln, U.S. Grant, Charles Dickens, and Mark Twain. The original Delmonico's restaurants would not survive the failed experiment of Prohibition. The Delmonico's that occupies the location today has no family connection to the original steakhouse, although it serves some of the same signature

Delmonico's Steakhouse. In 1891 the structure was restored into the triangular eight story building of today.

dishes, classics like Lobster Newburgh, while the Pompeii pillars still mark the entrance.

THE END OF AN ERA

By 1913, Buffalo Bill's hard and extravagant living had clearly taken its toll. The old scout had to be helped into the saddle, and a new form of entertainment was dawning: the motion picture. Cody's *Wild West Show* went bankrupt in 1913, and although Cody would make more appearances, and even try to get into the motion picture business, the era of *The Wild West Show* was over.

After a short battle with illness, William F. Cody passed away at his sister's home in Colorado on January 10, 1917, just short of his 71st birthday. Of course, Buffalo Bill's story couldn't end there. Cody's will, written in 1906, specified that he wanted to be buried on top of Cedar Mountain in Wyoming, overlooking the town he helped form and that bore his name, Cody. Lulu insisted that her departed husband wanted to be buried on Lookout Mountain outside Golden, Colorado. When it was announced that Cody, Wyoming's founding father was to be buried in Colorado, the citizens of Cody were not too happy. It was rumored that Lulu had accepted $10,000 from the publisher of a Golden Colorado newspaper to secure Buffalo Bill's internment in the Centennial State. The good citizens of Cody periodically threatened to steal the body, but the Coloradans were taking no chances with their famous corpse. Today, Buffalo Bill Cody rests in eternal peace on Lookout Mountain, with Lulu, and several tons of cement, on top of him.

Although he undoubtedly had feet of clay, Buffalo Bill Cody brought the Wild West to the hometowns of generations of enthusiastic spectators throughout the world. Not only did he bridge the gap from dime novels to motion pictures, he was also the genuine article, a showman of the highest order who first got bit by the showbiz bug on the stage of New York's Bowery Theater in 1872.

Samuel Clemens, c. 1867 (Courtesy of Library of Congress LC-USZ62-28851).

MARK TWAIN

*"I have taken a liking to the abominable place,
and every time I get ready to leave, I put it off a day or so,
from some unaccountable cause. It is as hard
on my conscience to leave New York,
as it was easy to leave Hannibal."*
SAMUEL LANGHORNE CLEMENS, OCTOBER 1853

A decade prior to adopting the nom de plume "Mark Twain," 17-year-old Samuel Clemens found himself in the largest city in the nation, beginning a love–hate relationship that would last his entire life. The young Mississippi River rat from Hannibal, Missouri was both drawn to and, to an extent, repulsed by the dichotomy between the opulent lifestyle of the enormously wealthy and the squalid living conditions of the working poor. In 1853, Clemens counted himself among the latter. He had secured modest employment as a typesetter at the publishing house of John A. Gray & Green located at 95-97 Cliff Street, on the southwest corner of Frankfort Street in lower Manhattan. He obtained lodging on Duane Street in today's trendy TriBeCa neighborhood, which he described as "a sufficiently villainous mechanics' boarding house ... ." Clemens would walk through part of the Five Points neighborhood on his daily commute, and its conditions certainly had not improved from Col. Crockett's visit almost 20 years earlier. Clemens later noted that "to wade through this mass of human vermin, would raise the ire of the most patient person that ever lived."

Although he spent only a couple of months in the city— he managed to see a play, *Gladiator*, at the old Broadway Theater at 326-328 Broadway—he often passed idle evening hours at the Free Printers Library at 3 Chambers Street. Clemens also visited America's first World's Fair, the 1853 World Exposition being held on Sixth Avenue and 42nd Street in what is now Bryant Park. The exhibits of the "industry of all nations" were housed in an enormous glass and cast-iron structure that had been christened the Crystal Palace, which Clemens found to be "a perfect fairy palace." The Crystal Palace's reign as New York's top tourist attraction was short lived; it was destroyed by fire in 1858 and never rebuilt.

Clemens soon left the Big City and returned to the Mississippi, but he would revisit New York more than a hundred times. He even spent most of his final years as a resident of New York City.

Sam worked odd jobs at different newspapers and printing shops in the Midwest. He also worked piloting Mississippi steamboats between St. Louis and New Orleans. The outbreak of the Civil War in 1861 put an abrupt end to his piloting career, and he spent about two weeks as a Confederate soldier in the Missouri militia. It remains unclear if the militia disbanded or if Sam simply quit; he would later quip that he resigned as a result of "fatigue through persistent retreating." In any event, his war was over, and he headed west.

In the middle of the nineteenth century, scores of the most talented journalists in the world followed the advice (whether he actually gave it or not) of Horace Greeley to "Go

Nagel & Weingarter lithograph of New York's Crystal Palace (Courtesy of Library of Congress LC-USZ-2341).

117

West." Sir Richard Burton, Washington Irving, Robert Louis Stevenson, Bret Harte, Helen Hunt Jackson, and, of course, Sam Clemens were among the hearty souls who eagerly chronicled the taming of the western frontier through novels and short stories, and by publishing newspapers in booming cow towns and rowdy mining camps. After a short, unsuccessful stint attempting to mine silver from the Comstock Lode in western Nevada, Clemens was offered a reporter's position at the Virginia City Daily *Territorial Enterprise* for $25 a week. As a reporter Clemens steadily developed his unique, humorous writing style and began using the pseudonym "Mark Twain," a name destined to become one of the most well-known in all of literature.

He moved on to San Francisco and visited some of the California gold fields, where he heard a campfire tale about a jumping frog, which he turned into a short story. Much to his surprise, "The Celebrated Jumping Frog of Calaveras County" reached a national audience when it was published by the *New York Saturday Press* in 1865. He would later turn his Western adventures into a lighthearted memoir, *Roughing It*. From there, Clemens, now Mark Twain, started to travel extensively, which he would do for the rest of his life, and would write dispatches to newspapers filled with his satirical observations and comical misadventures.

The Cooper Union
In May 1867, Twain would return to New York and give a "serio-humourous lecture" on his travels to the Hawaiian Islands at New York's famed Cooper Union, located at Cooper Square on Third Avenue between East 7th and East 8th Streets in New York's East Village. It was his stage debut in the East,

The Cooper Union today.

119

Michael P. O'Connor

*The Sioux Chief Red Cloud in the Great Hall of the Cooper Union,
surrounded by the Indian delegation of Braves and Squaws addressing
a New York audience on the wrongs done to his people, July 2, 1870
(Courtesy of Library of Congress LC-USZ62-10774).*

and he feared that New Yorkers would not pack the largest
venue in the city just to see him. He was more than pleas-
antly surprised when the hall was full and the enthusiastic
audience "laughed and shouted" for the entire hour and a
half. Twain left the Great Hall confident that his blossom-
ing career as a lecturer was also appreciated beyond the

West. He would continue to hone his public-speaking skills over the coming decades. His talent for the craft would make him the most famous and highest-paid lecturer in the world.

The Cooper Union is a privately funded college that was founded in 1859 and counts among its illustrious alumni the inventor Thomas Edison. The brownstone Foundation Building houses in its basement the Great Hall, which has been the venue for scores of political speeches, including 1860 presidential candidate Abraham Lincoln's historic "right makes might" speech made before an audience of 1,500 New Yorkers. Throughout the next century, the Great Hall would be the venue for scores of notable speakers, including Frederick Douglas, Ulysses S. Grant, Theodore Roosevelt, and, in 1870, the Lakota Sioux Chief Red Cloud.

St. Nicholas Hotel
In December 1867, Twain was back in New York and went to visit a friend at the St. Nicholas Hotel on Broadway, between Broome and Spring Streets. In the dining room of the grand hotel, his friend introduced him to his sister, Olivia Langdon. He was immediately smitten by the "sweet and timid and lovely young girl." The pair would marry within two years. On the December evening he met Olivia, he jumped at the opportunity to accompany her and her brother to Steinway Hall on 14th Street to hear Charles Dickens read from his new novel, *David Copperfield*.

The St. Nicholas Hotel was built in 1853 for the astronomical sum, at least for the time, of $1 million. Its primary purpose was to accommodate travelers attending the World Exposition. In 1854, the *New York Daily Tribune* reported that "it [was] said to be the largest and most elegant hotel in the

St. Nicholas Hotel mid 19th Century (Courtesy of New York Public Library).

world ... with the handsomest marble front in New York."
When Twain visited in 1867, the 350-room hotel was still
in its heyday and a particular favorite of Western tourists.
In just 30 years, however, the elegant hotel would fall out
of style, another victim of the theaters' uptown migration
to Union Square. In 1884, the hotel's furnishings were auctioned off, and most of the once-huge building was quickly
demolished. Surprisingly, a portion of the old St. Nicholas

Part of old St. Nicholas that still exists at 521-523 Broadway.

still exists at 521 and 523 Broadway, although the white marble has been painted over and iron fire escapes cover the entire front of the buildings. (opposite)

After Twain's triumphant debut at the Cooper Union, there would be no looking back. He would be a much sought-after and highly paid lecturer for the rest of his life, and he would return to New York City many times.

In the 1870s, while in the city, Twain would often stay in hotels by Madison Square Park, which had emerged as the theater district. He favored the Gilsey House, an eight-story, 300-room hotel built in 1872. The cast-iron hotel,

Hotel Gilsey c. 1916 (Courtesy of Library of Congress LC-USZ62-74597).

Restored Gilsey House at 1200 Broadway and East 29th Street.

with elegant dormers and an extraordinary three-storied mansard roof, thrived for three decades, attracting such prominent guests as Diamond Jim Brady and Oscar Wilde. The luxurious rooms featured rosewood and walnut finishing, as well as marble fireplace mantles.

However, when the theater district moved north, like so many other hotels, the Gilsey House fell out of favor and into disrepair. Fortunately, in the 1980s, the hotel was converted to co-op apartments and underwent major renovations. Today, the fully restored Gilsey House is a high-end co-op building that houses 40 apartments. It is located at 1200 Broadway and East 29th Street.

In the mid-nineteenth century, when Twain was in town, he liked to avail himself of adult beverages at Pfaff's Beer Cellar at 647 Broadway, near Bleecker Street. The basement beer hall attracted a bohemian crowd, including the great Walt Whitman, who wrote an unfinished poem, "The Two Vaults," about his favorite watering hole. Through the

647 Broadway (Pfaff's), with red awning.

years, Pfaff's Beer Cellar operated out of several locations, but the original location at 647 Broadway still survives as apartments and retail stores.

AN UNLIKELY FRIENDSHIP

In the spring of 1884, General Ulysses S. Grant, the former President of the United States, was flat broke. In 1883, Grant had invested $100,000, most of it borrowed, in his son's Wall Street brokerage house. The firm, Grant & Ward, went bankrupt, Ward went to prison, and the former General of the Army and Commander-in-Chief was left penniless. At the time, Grant was living in a stately brownstone at 3 E. 66th Street, between Fifth and Madison Avenues. A frequent visitor to the house was Mark Twain, and the men, one an old Union Commanding General and the other a former Confederate, became close friends. Twain convinced Grant to write his memoirs, and Twain would publish the book through his own publishing company, Charles L. Webster and Co. Around the same time, Grant discovered he had terminal throat cancer, which only reinforced his determination to finish the book. Grant wrote most of the memoirs at 3 E. 66th Street, with Twain often in attendance providing guidance and moral support. Grant succumbed to his illness on July 23, 1885, while at a cottage on Mt. McGregor in the Adirondacks, just days after finishing the book. The two-volume *Personal Memoirs of Ulysses S. Grant* was a literary and financial success, the book earning enough royalties to pay off all Grant's debts and provide financial security to Grant's widow, Julia, for the rest of her life.

The Brownstone at 3 E. 66th Street was razed in 1928 to make way for a nine-story apartment building, which now bears a plaque noting the site as the former residence of President Ulysses S. Grant.

In September 1887, Mark Twain took the train from his home in Hartford, Connecticut to meet the Scottish novelist Robert Louis Stevenson, whose theatrical adaption of Dr. Jekyll was playing on Broadway. Twain called on Stevenson at his hotel, the Hotel St. Stephen, at 23 E. 10th Street in Greenwich Village. The authors walked around nearby Washington Square Park, the two finally settling on a bench in the sunny northwest corner. They would speak for hours, apparently unrecognized.

The five-story St. Stephen Hotel, built in 1875–76, adjoined an apartment building on University Place that in 1887 was converted into the Hotel Albert. By the 1890s, the two hotels merged and took the name of the Hotel Albert. In 1901, Twain would give a lecture there to the Male Teachers' Association. For a hundred years, the Hotel Albert served as host to a large variety of artists, authors, musicians, and, in its later years, social radicals. Walt Whitman, Augustus St. Gaudens, Jackson Pollock, John Thomas Scopes, Rocky Graziano, and Thomas Wolfe were among its diverse patrons. In the 1960s, the Hotel Albert was a haven for musicians. At the hotel, The Mamas & The Papas wrote "California Dreamin'" and Lovin' Spoonful wrote "Do You Believe in Magic." Musicians including Jim Morrison, Carly Simon, Joni Mitchell, Otis Smith, and James Taylor used the hotel's basement for rehearsals and jam sessions.

Happily, the buildings still survive as co-ops (The Albert Apartment Corporation). The original Hotel Albert is located at the southeast corner of University Place and East 11th Street (Building C). The old Hotel St. Stephen, minus its

The Hotel Albert, c. 1907 (Courtesy of the Museum of the City of New York).

original facade, is located at 46-52 East 11th Street (Building D). Building B, on University Place, was an addition to the Hotel Albert in 1903, and Building A on the northeast corner of University Place and East 10th Street was an addition to the hotel in 1924.

In 1884, dissatisfaction with his publishers led Twain to start the publishing firm Charles L. Webster & Co., housed at 67 Fifth Avenue. Initially, Grant's memoirs and Twain's own works, including *The Adventures of Huckleberry Finn*, made the business money, but other publishing ventures

The Albert Apartment Complex today.

The legendary Players Club that overlooks Gramarcy Park.

did not fare as well. By April 1894, Twain, deep in debt, finally filed for bankruptcy. *The New York World* reported, "Mark Twain loses all." Twain, always susceptible to get-rich-quick schemes, had already experienced financial setbacks and had been spending considerable time in Europe. He returned to New York to wade through his latest financial disaster, and he did so at The Players, located at 16 Gramercy Park South, along a stretch of East 20th Street. Gramercy Park is a small two-acre park that opened in 1832 and still remains the only private park in New York City. The Players was a private social club founded in 1888 by the renowned Shakespearean actor Edwin Booth, and some of his equally famous friends, including Mark Twain and General William T. Sherman. The private club was unlike anything else in the country; it attracted prominent men from such varied professions as the arts, law, politics, publishing, and finance. Grover Cleveland, J. Pierpont Morgan, Cornelius Vanderbilt II, and Frederic Remington were among the park's elite membership. Edwin Booth, the brother of Lincoln's assassin, John Wilkes Booth, lived in an upstairs bedroom and would die there on June 7, 1893. A framed check to Grant's widow for $200,000, claimed by Twain to be the largest book royalty ever paid, hung on the wall for years. Today, the Greek-revival brownstone still houses the legendary Players Club that overlooks Gramercy Park (above).

THE BELLE OF NEW YORK
Although Twain was making a lot of money as a writer and lecturer, by 1895, his poor investments left him basically insolvent. To recoup his finances, he embarked on a worldwide lecture tour and successfully paid back all his debts.

The Wild West Meets the Big Apple

During the 1890s, despite financial setbacks and personal tragedy (he lost his oldest daughter to meningitis in 1896), Twain continued to spend a lot of time in New York. He was a frequent guest of honor at various social functions, which took place at such locations as the New York Press Club, the Century Club, and Loto's Club, the invitations earning him the nickname "The Belle of New York." It was somewhat ironic that such an ardent critic of the robber barons and excesses of the "gilded age" (he coined the phrase) would so relish the New York nightlife. Nevertheless, he did, and in 1900 Twain, having regained financial solvency, moved to New York City.

Twain and his family leased a brownstone at 14 W. 10th Street, off Fifth Avenue, from 1900 to 1901 (page 134), less than 10 blocks from where Butch Cassidy and the Sundance Kid caroused at Taylor's Boarding House at 234 W. 12th Street. These were happy times for Twain, and his daughter later recalled, "One could never describe the atmosphere of adulation that swept across the threshold." The brownstone still stands today, housing about 10 apartments. In a somber side note, the building was the site where attorney Joel Steinberg, in a drug-fueled rage, savagely beat a 6-year-old girl to death in 1987. Residents of the area have claimed that the building is haunted, and that Mark Twain's ghost occasionally makes an unobtrusive appearance.

In 1901, Twain moved his family to Wave Hill, a gray field-stone mansion situated on 28 acres overlooking the Hudson River, in the Riverdale section of the Bronx. In the 1870s, Teddy Roosevelt's family had leased it as a summer retreat. Today, Wave Hill consists of public gardens and a cultural center, and visitors can tour the old house.

Twain and his family leased this brownstone at 14 West 10th Street, off Fifth Avenue from 1900 to 1901.

Twain suffered a devastating loss in 1904 when his wife and lifelong traveling companion, Livy, died while the couple was in Europe. The heartbroken Twain moved back to New York City, leasing a brick townhouse at 21 Fifth Avenue, at the corner of East 9th Street, a couple hundred yards from Washington Square. The Romanesque Revival-style home was designed by the noted architect James

Renwick Jr., who also designed St. Patrick's Cathedral. The author Washington Irving had also lived there for a while in the 1850s. Twain spent a lot of time in the home playing billiards in the basement, and he started dictating his autobiography while propped in a four-post bed in his downstairs bedroom.

Mark Twain at home c. 1905

To the outside world, Mark Twain, with his mop of white hair and walrus mustache, dressed in his signature white flannel suit and smoking a strong black cigar, was still very much the Belle of New York. Twain seemingly reveled in his celebrity, calling himself "the most conspicuous man on the planet." The New York press, anxious for a humorous quote, faithfully followed his social appearances at venues like Madison Square Garden, The Players, and Delmonico's Steakhouse on 44th Street and Fifth Avenue, where New York's elite threw him a 70th birthday dinner on December 5, 1905.

Despite outward appearances, Twain never recovered emotionally from his beloved wife's passing, and in 1906 he was dealt a further blow when his youngest daughter, Jean, had to be institutionalized for severe epilepsy. Twain would later say of his Fifth Avenue home, "[W]hen I am not away from home I live in bed, to beat the lonesomeness …. [N]obody thrives in this house. Nobody profits from it except the doctors." Twain moved out of the Fifth Avenue house in 1908 and relocated to Redding, Connecticut, where he lived the remainder of his life.

The four-story architectural gem at 21 Fifth Avenue became known as the "Mark Twain House" and survived demolition attempts into the 1950s. Progress could be delayed but not stopped, however, and in 1954, the Mark Twain House and four other pre-Civil War townhouses, along with the nearby historic Brevoort Hotel, were razed to make way for what *The New York Times* called a "tall ultramodern Apartment building," which today is the 20-story Brevoort Co-op Apartment complex.

Twain only lasted another couple of years at his estate, "Stormfield," but life dealt him one more cruel turn when his daughter Jean suffered a heart attack during a seizure and drowned in the bathtub on Christmas Eve 1909. Less than six months later, on April 21, 1910, Samuel Langhorne Clemens, and the character he created, the writer, lecturer, and raconteur Mark Twain, passed away at home from a short bout of illness, and a broken heart.

On April 23, 1910, over 3,000 people passed in front of his open coffin during the funeral services held at the Brick Presbyterian Church (demolished in 1938) on Fifth Avenue and 37th Street. The New York Times lamented, "[Twain's] personality and his humor have been an integral part of American life for so long that it has seemed almost impossible to realize an America without him."

Although Samuel Clemens belonged to America, and his contributions enriched the entire world, many of the events that shaped his life occurred in New York City: his first job in publishing; the launching of his lecturing career; the meeting of his bride of 34 years; and, most importantly, many of the happiest moments of his life, all of them happened in the Big Apple. As Mark Twain wily observed, "Make your mark in New York, and you are a made man."

George Armstrong Custer and his devoted Libbie during the Civil War years (Courtesy of Library of Congress LC-BH831-702).

THE LITTLE LADIES

Elizabeth Bacon Custer

On June 30, 1876, at Fort Abraham Lincoln in North Dakota, 34-year-old Elizabeth "Libbie" Custer received the devastating report that her husband, Lt. Col. George Armstrong Custer and his entire immediate command had been killed by Sioux and Lakota warriors on the grassy slopes of the Little Bighorn River in Montana. In all, 268 soldiers and civilians perished in the Battle of the Little Bighorn, including 27 New Yorkers, the most of any state. The shocked and heartbroken Libbie, nonetheless, fulfilled her duty as a commander's wife and personally delivered the sad news to the new widows of Custer's troopers.

Modern historians and Custer buffs still argue whether the Civil War's "Boy General" bears responsibility for the military debacle that became known as "Custer's Last Stand." There was, however, no such debate in the eyes of Libbie Custer, who dedicated the rest of her long life to preserving the memory of her husband as a brave and dashing soldier sacrificed for the cause of Manifest Destiny.

139

Libbie would go on to write three books on her experiences in the West, all of them proclaiming the virtues of her "Autie." Libby did more than write books, though. She lectured throughout the country, raised funds for memorials, and fought for higher pensions for military widows. Libbie firmly believed that the best defense is a good offense, and she relentlessly defended Custer's questionable tactics at the Little Bighorn by affirmatively and passionately keeping Custer in the public eye. Libbie let anyone who would listen know that her husband had been a courageous military commander who fought a heroic battle against overwhelming odds. She unabashedly referred to herself as "the widow of a national hero."

Libbie became a sought-after speaker and popular fundraiser, and she traveled throughout the country defending Custer's legacy. In the 1890s, she settled in Westchester County, where she made her home until 1924 when she moved into a new cooperative apartment building at 71 Park Avenue, between 38th and 39th Streets.

In their heyday, Libbie and her famous husband had enjoyed the New York City nightlife. Their last visit to the city together spanned the winter of 1875 into February 1876. They attended the theater and were popular guests at dinners and social receptions. They stayed at the Hotel Brunswick, located on the northern end of Madison Square Park, until the money got tight and they moved across the street to a rented room.

Once she relocated to Park Avenue, on sunny days, the elderly Libbie made a ritual of walking the city streets. On Thursday afternoons, she habitually walked to the Cosmopolitan Club, on 44th Street and Lexington Avenue. She would occasionally lecture to fellow club members about her frontier and wartime experiences, and, of course, about her beloved Autie.

On April 4, 1933, Elizabeth Bacon Custer passed away quietly in her ninth-floor apartment, just two days short of her 91st birthday. The next day, *The New York Times* noted that her apartment was filled with mementos and

71 Park Avenue today.

141

relics of her famous husband's military exploits, including the Confederate flag of truce from Appomattox. It would only be after Libby's passing that her husband's actions at the Little Bighorn would be the subject of open criticism. However, by then, the image of Custer heroically posed on Last Stand Hill, fighting to the last against overwhelming odds, had been firmly imbedded in the American psyche. Libbie Custer had once again done her duty.

The red stucco 13-story apartment building at the prestigious 71 Park Avenue address still stands today.

Josephine Marcus Earp

On October 26, 1881, the Old West's quintessential gunfight played out in the silver-mining boomtown of Tombstone, Arizona. Wyatt Earp, his brothers Virgil and Morgan, and the alcoholic loose-cannon Doc Holliday walked down Fremont Street into the vacant lot behind the O.K. Corral, and into Western mythology as well. There they faced down the Clantons and McLaurys. After 30 seconds of gunfire, two Clantons and a McLaury were dead. Virgil, Morgan, and the world's meanest dentist were wounded. Wyatt emerged from the shootout unscathed, and with a woman who would be his companion for the rest of his life: Josephine Sarah "Sadie" Marcus, a native New Yorker.

Historians disagree on what brought the beautiful Josephine to Tombstone. By some accounts, Josephine went there with an acting troupe and stayed when she became romantically involved with the sheriff, Johnny Behan. It has also been surmised that Josephine had been a prostitute involved with Behan, and that she followed him to Tombstone. In any event, Josephine's amorous relationship with Behan fueled

Josephine Sarah Marcus, c. 1881. Photograph taken by noted Tombstone photographer C.S. Fly.

the already existing animosity between him and Earp, who was smitten with the buxom 22-year-old.

By the fall of 1881, a political power struggle between ranchers and the Earp brothers over control of Tombstone had reached its boiling point. The Earps, though lawmen by trade, had their hands in various financial dealings, including Tombstone's gambling, saloons, and prostitution. The ranchers, called cowboys, had questionable methods of obtaining cattle and resented the Earps, whom they viewed as Northern carpetbaggers. It was this tension that led to the famous duel. Josephine later wrote, and Hollywood would enthusiastically portray, that as the gun smoke cleared, she ran past Behan and embraced Wyatt, relieved her true love was alive. Although not involved in the gunfight, Behan had been aligned with the town's anti-Earp faction and unsuccessfully attempted to arrest Wyatt after the shootout. Wyatt, reportedly, responded cooly, "I won't be arrested now."

Wyatt, his brothers, and Doc Holliday ultimately were arrested and charged with murder, but after a preliminary hearing it was determined that there was insufficient evidence to indict. The saga of the gunfight at O.K. Corral did not end there, however. The cowboys, seeking revenge, ambushed and severely wounded Virgil Earp, and on March 18, 1882, Morgan Earp was shot and killed while playing billiards in a saloon.

The enraged Wyatt secured an appointment as a Deputy U.S. Marshal and formed a posse, commencing his bloody Vendetta Ride to avenge the assaults on his brothers. For three weeks, the Earp posse scoured Arizona Territory for the cowboys, and it is believed that as many as 16 were killed. When the killing spree ended, Wyatt, by now a wanted man himself, left Arizona Territory for good.

Modern historians view with a critical eye Earp's popular media portrayal. Films such as *My Darling Clementine* and the long-running television program from the late 1950s *The Life and Legend of Wyatt Earp*, depicted Earp as a virtuous lawman cleaning up the most violent towns in the Old West. In truth, Earp's character wasn't so morally pure. His critics are quick to point out his faults and less than exemplary business interests. While Wyatt was certainly a complicated man, he clearly was not a man to be trifled with.

After the Vendetta Ride, Wyatt drifted to New Mexico and Colorado, and by the end of 1882 was in San Francisco, where he met up with Josephine. By that time, Wyatt had dispatched to his parents his common-law wife, Mattie, and would spend the next half century with Josephine. They traveled together to boomtowns throughout the West, and even to Alaska. The childless pair eventually settled in Los Angeles, where Wyatt diligently, but unsuccessfully, tried to peddle his memoirs to publishers. He would also hang out in Hollywood backlots, befriending the likes of silent-film star William S. Hart and director John Ford.

The aging Wyatt also took a liking to a USC football player who was trying to break into the movie business by working as a prop man. The aspiring actor, Marion Morrison, would get his break in time, and the world would get to know him by his more familiar name: John Wayne.

Prior to passing away in 1929, at the age of 80, Wyatt had begun talking to author Stuart Lake, who had expressed an interest in writing Wyatt's biography. Upon Wyatt's death, Josephine continued the dialogue with Lake to ensure that her beloved Wyatt was painted in the right light. The resulting book, *Wyatt Earp: Frontier Marshal*, was published in 1931 and became a best seller. It was also a work of complete fiction. Despite its complicated relationship with the truth, the book would serve as the basis of the Wyatt Earp legend and the foundation for Earp's growth into the preeminent symbol of frontier justice preserved in countless movies and television shows through the decades. Josephine had a strong influence on Lake's book and managed to omit any mention of her even being in Tombstone, let alone of the love triangle between her and the two lawmen. In fact, Josephine is only mentioned once in the entire biography, though even that claim, that she and Wyatt were married in San Francisco, is untrue. For the remainder of her life, Josephine would keep a sharp eye out for any publication or film that even planned to mention Wyatt Earp. If she did not approve the content, she would threaten litigation. Her diligence worked. The sanitized version of the legend of Wyatt Earp has endured for decades.

Josephine, who, despite her influence, was not completely satisfied with the Lake book and decided to transcribe her own memoirs, which in 1976 were published as *I Married Wyatt Earp, The Recollections of Josephine Sarah Marcus Earp*. The work was credited as having been collected and edited by Glenn G. Boyer. In theory, Boyer had access to Josephine's working manuscript. In reality, however, it is unclear if Boyer ever had such access, and the book is riddled with factual inaccuracies; even the cover photograph has been proven to picture someone other than Josephine. Consequently, it has been difficult for historians and Earp enthusiasts to separate fact from fiction in researching the lives of Wyatt and Josephine. Earp researchers go into an academic tizzy if either the Boyer or Lake books are cited as references.

Josephine Earp would continue to safeguard Wyatt's image for the rest of her life, which would last until 1944. Her remains are buried next to Wyatt's, in a Jewish cemetery in Colma, California.

Although it is difficult to piece together Josephine's early pedigree because of the suspect biographies, there is no doubt that she was born in New York City in 1860 to Sophia Lewis and Hyman (Henry) Marcus, Jewish immigrants from

Prussia. Although, no birth records have ever been located for Josephine, the first time she appears in a census is 1870, by which time her family had moved to San Francisco, and her place of birth was noted as New York. In 1860, a large Jewish population had settled in Manhattan's Lower East Side, which is her likely birthplace. It is also know that when she had been working on her memoirs, she contacted New York City offices in an unsuccessful attempt to obtain her birth certificate.

It is hard to overestimate Josephine's impact on both the Old West's history and its enduring image in American culture. Josephine Sarah Marcus Earp was not only present at the Gunfight at the O.K. Corral but was also a contributing factor in escalating the tensions in Tombstone that led to the volatile shootout. In her later years, her insistent safeguarding of Wyatt's reputation resulted in the development of the prototypical image of the Western lawman as vigilant, selfless, and fearless, an archetype that would be a staple in the media for the next 75 years.

1856 lithograph of John C. Fremont (Courtesy of Library of Congress LC-USZ62-107503).

OLD SOLDIERS FADING AWAY

Major General John C. Fremont

Although the name John C. Fremont does not immediately come to mind when contemplating Western personalities, one would be hard pressed to find another individual whose career intertwined more closely with pivotal periods in the expansion and ultimate settling of the West.

Fremont was born in 1813. He earned the nickname "The Pathfinder" for having led five successful topographic expeditions through the Rocky Mountains from 1842 to 1854, seeking overland routes from the Mississippi to the Pacific. In addition to preparing maps and surveys, Fremont was tasked with making Western travel, and the West itself, seem as alluring as possible. Fremont's father-in-law was Missouri Senator Thomas Hart Benton, a Washington insider and vocal advocate of Western expansion. Fremont's faithful guide and lifelong friend for these expeditions was none other than the famed scout and Indian fighter Kit Carson. Fremont by chance had met the venerable mountain man on a Missouri River steamboat in 1842. In the coming years, there is little doubt it would be Carson who would find most, if not all, of the paths for the Great Pathfinder. It didn't matter to Carson, who was more than happy to avoid the limelight (although he would ultimately become one of the most famous men in America). The two men formed a strong bond and mutual respect, their relationship forged from years spent together overcoming the harsh and perilous elements of the Rocky Mountains. Carson would later recall, "[It was] impossible to describe the hardships through which we passed, nor am I capable of doing justice to the credit which Fremont deserves. I can never forget his treatment of me while I was in his employ, and how cheerfully he suffered with his men." High praise from the great Kit Carson.

At the outbreak of the Mexican-American War in 1846, Lt. Fremont, either by fortune or by design, found himself in California, where, through a series of minor engagements, he declared California free of Mexico and himself military governor. He was later court-martialed for refusing to abdicate his authority to the American commander, and subsequently resigned from the Army.

Fremont continued his expeditions, and the Gold Rush of 1849 made him a multimillionaire. Through his wife, Jessie, and Senator Benton, Fremont throughout his life cultivated and maintained highly influential political connections. In 1850, Fremont was elected Governor of California, and in 1856 he unsuccessfully ran against James Buchanan as the first Republican candidate for president.

In 1861, with the outbreak of the Civil War, Fremont was once again called to arms. He was appointed a Major General in the Union and placed in command of the newly created Western Department. Characteristically, General Fremont soon ran into political trouble when he autocratically declared free all slaves owned by Confederates in Missouri. President Lincoln, desperately trying to keep border states in the Union, told Fremont to modify the order. Fremont refused and was promptly removed from command. The politically astute Fremont once again landed on his feet and was appointed commander of the Mountain Department of the Army. Fremont's performance was less than spectacular, and he ended up spending most of the war behind a desk in New York City.

Fremont, again employing his political savvy, served as Territorial Governor of Arizona from 1878 until 1881, surprisingly without controversy. Fremont and his wife ultimately retired to the New York City area, in an attempt to earn back his fortune, which he had lost through a series of poor investments. The General and Jessie spent some time in Westchester County and Staten Island before finally settling into a long-since demolished townhouse at 49 W. 25th Street, between Sixth Avenue and Broadway. On July 13, 1890, The Pathfinder passed away in his residence after a short but fatal bout of peritonitis. The well-attended funeral was held at St. Ignatius Chapel at 54-56 W. 40th Street, where General William Sherman served as one of the pallbearers. St. Ignatius has since moved to the Upper West Side, but the old church building facing Bryant Park still stands, although it has gone through some reincarnations, including the headquarters for Daytop Village.

General William Tecumseh Sherman
William Tecumseh Sherman earned his fame (or infamy, depending on your geographical location in relation to the

Contemporary Photo. 54-56 West 40th Street across from Bryant Park which once housed St. Inganious Church, site of funeral of Gen. John C. Fremont.

Mason Dixon line) during the Civil War. In November 1864, after conquering Atlanta, Sherman lead his 62,000 troops to Savannah on a "March to the Sea." Sherman left in his wake a 285-mile path of destruction and misery. His stated purpose was "to make Georgia howl" by destroying its infrastructure and, maybe more importantly, undermining civilian morale. His "total war" tactics clearly hastened the end of the Confederacy, but they also foretold the devastating future of warfare for the next century.

Tecumseh Sherman was born on February 20, 1820 in Lancaster, Ohio, into an affluent family, his father being an Ohio Supreme Court Justice. Tragically, his father died

1883 photograph of Gen. Sherman (Courtesy of Library of Congress LC-USZ62-53470).

when the lad was just 9 years old. He was taken in and raised by a family friend, Thomas Ewing, an Ohio Senator. The Catholic Senator Ewing gave Tecumseh the Christian name of William and secured for his foster son an appointment to West Point in 1836. While at the Academy, the studious Sherman would go to New York City as often as his cadet obligations would allow. He saw his first theatrical performance at the Park Theater in July 1837, which began his lifelong passion for the performing arts.

Upon graduating in 1840, Sherman embarked on a somewhat lackluster military career. Much to his dismay, unlike many of his soon-to-be-famous contemporaries, the future general did not see action during the Mexican-American War, serving instead in California during the heady gold rush days. In 1850, he married Eleanor (Ellen) Ewing, the daughter of Senator Ewing, his foster father. That same year, convinced that his lack of combat experience had stymied his military career, Sherman resigned from the Army. He would go on to try his hand in a variety of fields. He unsuccessfully attempted to practice law in Kansas, and in 1857 moved to New York City to run the New York branch of the bank Lucas and Co., located at 12 Wall Street. His banking career abruptly ended within a few months as a result of the Banking Panic of 1857, a worldwide financial crisis.

In 1861, at the dawning of the Civil War, Sherman found himself as a superintendent of the Seminary of Learning of the State of Louisiana, the predecessor to Louisiana State University. Sherman was somewhat torn in that, strikingly, he was not opposed to the "peculiar institution" of slavery. Despite his initial reluctance, Sherman realized where his duty laid, and ultimately secured a commission as a colonel in the Union Army. Sherman was not caught up in the patriot fever sweeping the North; he had spent a significant amount of time in the South and was throughly convinced that Northern politicians and military officers were severely underestimating the capabilities of the Confederate forces, and particularly their will and ability to fight.

Sherman was quickly promoted to Brigadier General, but adamantly, relentlessly, and continuously complained to anyone who would listen about Union shortages in men and supplies. This nearly constant agitation led to Sherman being relieved of his command. Newspapers proclaimed that he was insane, and his wife didn't help by noting that insanity ran in the Sherman family. In retrospect, it appears that Sherman was simply, and perhaps justifiably, having a nervous breakdown. In Sherman's defense, his ominous predictions concerning the unprecedented bloodshed yet to come would prove accurate.

Within a couple of months, he was back in the saddle. Sherman's destiny, if not that of the nation, changed when he was was placed under the immediate command of U.S. Grant in the Army of West Tennessee. After losing a devastating battle at Shiloh, the Army of West Tennessee bounced back and secured critical victories at Vicksburg and Chattanooga. The troops under Sherman's command affectionally called him "Uncle Billy" because of his visible, heartfelt concern for their welfare and unpretentious style; he was known to wear his uniform, a custom made product of New York's Brooks Brothers, crumpled, its bespoke origins well hidden from his men.

When U.S. Grant was given command of the Army of the Potomac, he hand picked Sherman to lead the Army of

West Tennessee, which proceeded to capture and utterly destroy the vital railroad and commercial center of Atlanta. With Atlanta in flames, General Sherman commenced his "March to the Sea."

At the end of the Civil War, Sherman was placed in command of the Division of the Missouri District, which stretched from the Mississippi River to the Rocky Mountains. This vast territory included the still adamantly defended Sioux and Cheyenne hunting grounds on the Northern Plains, the Southern Plains, home to the Kiowas and Comanches, and the mountain strongholds of the Apaches in New Mexico. General Sherman now turned his attention to the "Indian problem." Settlers, railroad workers, and miners pouring into the West needed protection, and, simply put, the Native Americans were in the way of Manifest Destiny.

Sherman now unleashed on the Native American tribes the same scorched-earth policy that had devastated and demoralized the South. Sherman's strategy was to put all Native Americans on reservations. He declared "that all Indians not on Reservations [were] hostile and [would] remain so until killed." He viewed the wholesale slaughter of the American Buffalo as a tactical means to destroy the Plains Indians' way of life and implemented winter attacks on Indian villages, when the tribes were at their most vulnerable.

In 1868, General Sherman met with Sioux Chief Red Cloud and signed the Fort Laramie Treaty. The treaty brought an end to Red Cloud's attacks along the Bozeman Trail (Red Cloud's War), which connected the gold-rush territory of Montana with the Oregon Trail, the major passage to the West Coast. The Bozeman Trail had been heavily used by miners but cut through plentiful buffalo grounds revered by several bands of the Lakota people. In turn, the Lakotas were guaranteed ownership of the Black Hills and additional land that was to be utilized as a reservation encompassing parts of South Dakota, Wyoming, and Montana. Although Sitting Bull would not sign the treaty, at the time it was seen as a victory for the Native Peoples because the U.S. Government also agreed to abandon its forts along the Bozeman Trail. The Fort Laramie Treaty would never be complied with by the government, and Red Cloud, although he remained an advocate for peace, would complain for the rest of his life that he was tricked into the treaty. At Red Cloud's Cooper Union speech on July 16, 1870, he lamented, "When you [Western settlers] first came we were many, and you were few; now you are many and we are getting very few, and we are poor." Red Cloud no doubt realized that the worst was yet to come.

When Sherman's friend and confidant U.S. Grant was elected president in 1869, he appointed Sherman General of the Army. In this position, he continued to devote significant efforts to making Western states safe for continued expansion. In this endeavor, he succeeded. Custer's shocking defeat at the Little Bighorn in 1876 would prove be the death knell for the Native American way of life. Sherman vowed that the Sioux "must feel the superior power of the Government." He intensified the Army's efforts to force what was left of the free-roaming Native American tribes onto reservations. The government totally disregarded The Treaty of Fort Laramie and by 1877 had seized the gold-rich Black Hills. Prior to his retirement from the Army in 1884, General Sherman surmised, "I now regard the the Indians as substantially eliminated from the problems of the Army." Although, through the coming years, there would be occasional flare ups, most significantly the Wounded Knee massacre in 1890, for the most part, Sherman's assessment was correct. The Trail of Tears that had started more than a half century before had finally reached its tragic end.

Although Sherman detested politics, and had avoided Washington as much as he possibly could during his long and distinguished military career, his name was bandied about as a Republican presidential candidate in 1884. He rejected the political overtures by promptly and succinctly responding, "I will not accept if nominated and will not serve if elected."

Sherman and his wife, Ellen, had planned to spend their retirement years in St. Louis, but in the fall of 1886 they moved to New York City. They wanted to be closer to their daughter Minnie, who was living in Pennsylvania, and their son Philemon, who was attending Yale University. The General, Ellen, and their two daughters, Rachel and Lizzie, settled into the Fifth Avenue Hotel, located at 200 Fifth Avenue, facing Madison Square Park from 23rd Street to 24th Street. The fashionable hotel was built in 1859 and was a particular favorite of politicians, including U.S. Grant and Chester A. Arthur. It was also the first hotel in the United States to install a passenger elevator. On December 11, 1872, tragedy struck the Fifth Avenue Hotel when a fire broke out on the top floor and claimed the lives of 15 of the hotel's employees.

Like the nearby Hoffman House, the Fifth Avenue Hotel fell on hard times at the turn of the century when the

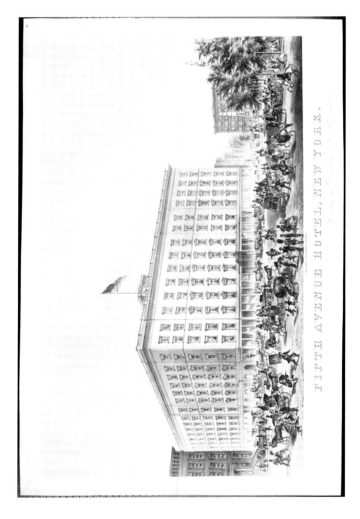

The Fifth Avenue Hotel, c. 1860 (Courtesy of the Museum of the City of New York).

159

entertainment district migrated northward. It was demolished in 1908.

Ellen wasn't thrilled about residing at the Fifth Avenue Hotel, and so relocated temporarily to New Jersey. It had been suspected that in 1880, the 60-year-old General had commenced an affair with 35-year-old Mary Audenreid, the

Site of old Fifth Avenue Hotel at 200 Fifth Avenue stretching from 23rd to 24th Street facing Madison Square Park.

widow of his former chief of staff, and that the Fifth Avenue Hotel provided the posh venue for their illicit liaisons.

In the fall of 1888, Sherman bought a house, which no longer stands, at 75 W. 71st Street, at the corner of 71st and Columbus Avenue, a block from Central Park. Unfortunately, Ellen, his spouse of 38 years, had been in declining health and passed away in the house shortly after moving in. The General went on to become a fixture of New York society. He was often seen at the theater and spent many evenings at The Players and the Union League Club, which was located at 26 E. 17th Street, near Broadway. In an 1891 letter to his brother, Sherman described his routine: "Dear Brother—I am drifting along in the old rut—in good strength, attending about four dinners out per week at public or private houses, and generally wind up for gossip at the Union League Club ... ."

On the evening of February 4, 1891, the General went out in severe weather to join friends at the Casino Theater, located at 1404 Broadway at West 39th Street. He woke the next morning with what he thought was a cold, but the symptoms steadily worsened. On February 14, the 71-year-old retired general passed away at his home. A private viewing took place there, and a funeral mass, presided over by his son Thomas, a Roman Catholic priest, was held at St. Patrick's Cathedral. Acting as an honorary pallbearer was former Confederate General Joseph Johnston, who had surrendered his command, including all Southern troops in the Carolinas, Georgia, and Florida, to General Sherman in 1865. Despite the cold and rainy weather, the crusty old general refused to wear a hat, foolishly believing it would be a sign of disrespect to his former foe. Standing on the steps of St. Patrick's Cathedral, Johnston brushed off inquiries concerning his health, illogically explaining, "[I]f I were in his place, and he were standing here in mine, he would not put on his hat." The result of Johnston's stubborn refusal to avail himself of headgear is that the 84-year-old caught pneumonia and died within a few weeks. New York's bitter February weather had claimed two battle-hardened veterans.

In any event, the hatless Johnston was among the mourners who left St. Patrick's and joined a military funeral procession consisting of 3,000 soldiers. The line of mourners then marched down Fifth Avenue to the tip of Manhattan,

Funeral procession of Gen. William T. Sherman (Courtesy of Museum of the City of New York).

162

escorting the General's remains to a ferry for transport to New Jersey, where the flag-draped coffin was loaded onto a specially outfitted Funeral Train bound for St. Louis. Tens of thousands lined up along Fifth Avenue to pay their final respects to a military hero and fellow New Yorker.

BUGLER JOHN MARTIN

When George Armstrong Custer surveyed the banks of the Little Big Horn River, he immediately surmised that he was greatly outnumbered. He called for his adjutant, Lt. Cooke, who quickly scribbled the General's orders:

Benteen

> Come on. Big Village
> Be Quick. Bring Packs

W.W. Cooke
P.S. Bring Packs.

Lt. Cooke handed the message to "the last white man to see Custer alive," bugler John Martin. Martin successfully made his way to Captain Frederick Benteen, but Benteen never made it to Custer's aid. In all likelihood, Benteen's failure to support Custer, although still a hotly debated issue, didn't matter; Custer and his command were quickly surrounded and overwhelmed within an hour. Benteen and the bulk of his command, along with Martin were spared.

Trooper John Martin was actually born Giovanni Crisotimo Martino in Italy in 1853 and immigrated to New York in 1873. He promptly enlisted in the U.S. Cavalry, and would spend the next 30 years in the Army.

Michael P. O'Connor

Bugler John Martin (Courtesy of Denver Public Library, Western History Collection).

Martin settled in Brooklyn in 1906, living at 168 Prospect Street, and worked as a "ticket chopper" at the 103rd Street station on the New York City Subway System for $45 a month. Prior to turnstiles, "ticket choppers" would take tickets from entering passengers and shred them. Martin would often play his bugle during intermissions of Broadway plays and would relish retelling his exploits on that fateful June day in 1876. On June 24, 1906, Martin was given the honor of playing "Taps" over Custer's grave at the United States Military Academy at West Point during a ceremony recognizing the 25th anniversary of the battle. In his later

164

years, he worked at the Brooklyn Navy Yard. On Christmas Eve 1922, Martin was struck by a beer truck on a Brooklyn street and died three days later at the age of 69. The old bugler was buried at a military cemetery at Cypress Hills in Brooklyn.

James Bowie, c. 1820. The only known oil painting of Jim Bowie from life (Courtesy of State of Texas Preservation Board).

JUST PASSIN' THROUGH

James Bowie

In 1833, James Bowie made a short excursion to New York City. It was not his first trip to the big city; he had been there on business in 1826 and 1828. By 1833, though, the 36-year-old knife fighter was a famous man, and one to be reckoned with. Bowie's fame, unlike David Crockett's, which was based primarily on tall tales and self-promotion, was based upon Bowie's ability to come out on top in deadly knife fights along the perilous Mississippi River, and for the killing instrument that bore his name. He was a smuggler and a slave trader who counted among his business associates the pirate Jean Laffite. It is easy to see why in 1955 Walt Disney selected Davy Crockett over Bowie as the TV hero to promote Frontierland in his soon-to-open amusement park.

Bowie ventured to New York City in 1833, along with his brother Rezin, who was suffering from failing eyesight and in search of a competent physician. James accompanied his older sibling to 25 Park Place to consult with eminent surgeon Dr. Valentine Mott. Dr. Mott's Park Place office was a

The 1857 building that still stands at 23-25 Park Place, the site of Dr. Mott's 1833 office.

three-story brownstone townhouse situated on the northwest side of the street between Broadway and Church Street. The structure was replaced in 1857 by a five-story party-wall building at 23 and 25 Park Place that extends through the block to 20 and 22 Murray Street. The 1857 building still stands today and in 2007 was designated as a Landmark Site by the New York City Landmarks Commission. In granting the building Landmark designation, the Commission noted that it was a "handsome example of the mid-nineteenth century double store and loft buildings."

It has been speculated that during the 1833 visit Rezin and James came in contact with the English merchants and importers John Graveley and Charles Wreaks. New York City directories indicate that in 1836 Graveley was a neighbor of Dr. Mott, living at 1 Park Place. In 1836 Wreaks and Graveley would form a partnership and become one of the country's premier importers and sellers of Bowie knives. The cutlery firm imported the custom-made knives from Sheffield, England and operated out of the Astor House on Broadway, where they maintained a showroom of elegantly mounted Bowie knives. In 2010, a coffin-hilt Bowie knife bearing a Graveley and Wreaks stamp sold at auction for over $25,000. In 1839, when the knife was first manufactured and sold, it would cost just $1.50.

While in New York, Bowie took a short stroll from Park Place to City Hall and observed a court proceeding involving an old foe, Col. Robert Crain. Crain had been a participant in the 1827 Sandbar Fight outside of Natchez, Mississippi. The Sandbar Fight was well-known throughout the Southwest. It had begun as a chivalrous duel but had quickly erupted into an all-out brawl that left two men dead and four others seriously wounded, including Bowie and Crain. Crain was in the New York courtroom attempting to obtain possession of a Black man he believed to be a runaway slave. Apparently, during testimony, Col. Crain made comments that many of the Northern observers found offensive, and the gallery was quickly turning into a mob. The imposing Jim Bowie, putting aside the fact that Crain had once shot him, quickly sprang to his fellow Southerner's defense, and the unruly crowd was promptly subdued.

Dr. Mott referred the brothers to a physician in Philadelphia, where Rezin ultimately had eye surgery. James then left the Northeast, destined never to return. Earlier that year, Bowie's young wife and two children had died during a cholera epidemic, and the tough knife fighter was never the same. His existing penchant for drinking and gambling increased, and he threw himself wholeheartedly behind the growing movement for Texas independence.

In February 1836, he shared an uneasy co-commandancy of the Alamo with Col. William Barret Travis. Travis' complaints about Bowie's drinking binges fell on the unreceptive ear of Sam Houston, himself no stranger to the cup that cheers. Bowie's partying came to an abrupt end when he succumbed to a "disease of a peculiar nature." The illness may have been tuberculosis, and Bowie was left bedridden. After the Alamo's siege on the morning of March 6, Bowie's mutilated body was found in his cot, where legend says he fought desperately, but ultimately unsuccessfully, with his deadly knife and a pair of pistols given to him by David Crockett. There are some historians who dispute the intensity of the fight Bowie put up, but it is hard to fathom that he did anything less than what the legend holds. When told of her son's demise, Mrs. Bowie coldly noted, "I'll wager they found no wounds in his back."

Robert Ford

Robert Ford, immortalized in song as the "dirty little coward" who shot Jesse James, catapulted into Western lore with his assassination of the popular outlaw on April 3, 1882 in St. Joseph, Missouri. Robert, along with his brother, Charley, had joined the dwindling James gang, but the allure of a $10,000 bounty being offered by the State of Missouri broke their tentative allegiance to Jesse.

Robert Ford, c. 1882, holding the pistol he used to kill Jesse James.

While having breakfast in his home with the Ford brothers, Jesse got up from the table and decided to straighten a picture hanging on the wall. Jesse then made the fatal error of standing on a chair to adjust the picture, turning his back on the Ford brothers. Robert stood from the table, cocked his pistol, and shot the 34-year-old Jesse James in the back of the head, killing him instantly.

Robert was only able to secure a small portion of the promised reward, so he decided to cash in on his celebrity status by taking his act on the road. Robert and Charley concocted a one-act play entitled *Outlaws of Missouri* that dramatized Robert's slaying of the notorious Western badman, with Charley reluctantly portraying the fallen James. Blatantly omitted from the melodrama was the fact that Robert had shot the unarmed Jesse from behind.

In September 1882, the Ford brothers were performing to lukewarm audiences at Bunnell's Museum in Brooklyn when Charley thought he spotted the wife of Frank James in the crowd. The duo reasoned that Frank, himself not a man to be trifled with, could not be far behind.

The Ford brothers crossed the East River and performed until the first week in October at the Broadway Museum, located at 1221 Broadway at 30th Street. The museum and theater had operated under several different owners since it started operation in 1867 as Wood's Museum. The building was demolished in 1920.

The Brother's acting careers did not last much longer, as audiences became more and more hostile to Robert's fanciful reenactment of the killing. Robert had clearly misjudged the popularity of Jesse James, and Robert would spend the rest of his life in fear, roaming from town to town to hide his shame. Fate caught up with Robert Ford on June 8, 1892, when a drifter named Edward O'Kelley walked into a dingy tent saloon in Creede, Colorado and blasted Ford into eternity with a double-barreled shotgun. The fatal blasts, in an ironic twist of fate, came from behind, leaving Ford and James, two men forever linked, slain in the same cruel and cowardly manner.

Sheriff Pat Garrett

Pat Garrett, sheriff of Lincoln County, New Mexico, entered the annals of Western lore on July 14, 1881, when he shot

Pat Garrett, c. 1899, Sheriff of Dona Ana County, New Mexico.

and killed the most infamous outlaw in American history, Billy the Kid. Garrett had been on the Kid's trail for close to a year—the Kid had slipped Garrett's grasp more than once—but the Kid's luck ran out that fateful summer night. He entered a darkened bedroom in a shack in Fort Sumner, New Mexico and found the determined Sheriff Garrett waiting for him. Garrett fired two shots, one striking the Kid in the heart. The exact sequence of events leading to the shooting are still much debated among historians and Kid enthusiasts, but one fact is clear: Billy the Kid was history, and it was Garrett that had made him so.

Although the circumstances were murky, Garrett was hailed as a hero. He was not immediately vilified in the manner of Robert Ford. Garret also didn't seek attention, and didn't want to be known only as the man who gunned down Billy the Kid. Garrett was a lawman, and Billy, although popular in the Mexican community of New Mexico, had worn out his welcome, whereas Jesse James was still viewed by many at the time of his death as a hero attempting to avenge the South's defeat in the Civil War.

Billy still had his sympathizers, however, and Garrett couldn't get reelected in New Mexico until 1899, when he was appointed Sheriff of Doña Ana County, New Mexico.

In 1901, President Theodore Roosevelt, infatuated with the West, appointed Garrett a United States Customs Collector at El Paso, Texas.

In July 1902, on Customs business, Pat Garrett ventured to New York City. Garrett stayed at the Marlborough Hotel in Herald Square, at the Northwest corner of Broadway and 36th Street. The elegant hotel, which boasted a "ladies restaurant," was razed in 1924. Garrett, always a natty dresser, shied away from wearing Western-style apparel. One evening, when he was out for a walk, he stopped a policeman and asked for directions back to the Marlborough Hotel. The officer looked the well-dressed tourist up and down and warned the bemused Garrett that "there is lots of fellows in this town looking for marks like you."

Garrett also went to Brooklyn's Coney Island, where he entertained the crowd with his marksmanship. The press reported that "Collector Pat Garrett of El Paso, Texas, six foot four in his stockings and afraid of no man who ever drew a gun will not be made welcome if he makes another trip to the shooting galleries at Coney Island." Garrett happily left with a box-and-a-half of cigars, and "he broke every clay pipe in site."

President Roosevelt did not reappoint Garrett during his second term, and in 1905 he returned to New Mexico, where he again tried his hand at ranching but spent the majority of his time drinking and gambling. On February 29, 1908, on a desolate stretch of road in Alameda Arroyo, a few miles east of Las Cruces, New Mexico, the killer of Billy the Kid was shot in the back of the head while relieving himself on the side of the road. The circumstances surrounding the killing are still shrouded in mystery, but thus ended the life of the man considered by many to be the greatest lawman of the Old West.

Print of the only known tintype of Billy the Kid (Courtesy of Library of Congress LC-USZ-136377).

WHAT ABOUT BILLY THE KID?

Without question, the most enduring legend of the Old West is Henry McCarty. The adventurous life of the baby-faced outlaw with the crooked smile captured the imagination of the American public over a century ago, and the myth of Billy the Kid remains as popular today. It has been estimated that over 60 motion pictures have featured a prominent Billy the Kid character, and he has been the principal subject in countless books, plays, and songs. In 2011, the only surviving tintype photograph of Billy the Kid sold at auction for a mind-boggling $2.3 million. Contemporary dime novels credited the Kid with 21 killings (one for each year he lived), although historians place the actual number at less than 10.

A generally accepted myth about Billy the Kid is that he entered life as Henry McCarty on November 23, 1859, in the predominately Irish slums of New York's Lower East Side. The mythical allure of such a humble and tough upbringing is obvious: the rough and tumble street-wise son of Irish immigrants heads west to seek his fame (or infamy) and fortune, the same as thousands of other Easterners.

Historians have called into question the veracity of the Kid's New York City heritage. Admittedly, there is a dearth of "hard" documentary evidence supporting the New York City birth thesis, although it should be kept in mind that the record-keeping in the mid-nineteenth century, especially among New York City's populous immigrant population, was not exhaustive. The genesis of the myth appears to come from the Kid's killer, Sheriff Pat Garrett, who wrote a biography, *The Authentic Life of Billy the Kid*, in which he claims that the Kid told him he was born on November 23, 1859 in New York City. The biography, factually questionable throughout, was written mostly by Garrett's drinking buddy, Ash Upton, whose birthday also happens to be November 23. Historians have surmised that this coincidence, in the absence of other evidence, is too great to be believed, thus casting the authenticity of the Kid's birthplace in doubt. Garrett's claim should not be rejected out of hand, however. Although Garrett exercised a liberal dose of poetic license to paint himself in the best possible light, he did indeed know the Kid fairly well. It is not beyond the realm of possibility that the Kid did, at some point, disclose his birthplace to Garrett.

In addition to Garret's assertion, there are bits and pieces of documentary evidence that support the proposition that Billy the Kid did indeed start his short but eventful life in the slums of New York City. For example, it should not be overlooked that contemporary newspaper accounts of the Kid's exploits, and ultimate death, routinely cited New York City as his place of birth.

Shortly after the Kid's death in 1881, *The New York Sun* reported that residents of New York's Fourth Ward, the impoverished Irish enclave, southeast of the Five Points, on the Lower East side, remembered young Henry McCarty and had no doubt that he was indeed Billy the Kid.

There are, however, other aspects of the Kid's origins that are accepted as factual. The Kid's mother, an Irish immigrant named Catherine McCarty, was born around 1829. She immigrated from Ireland in the 1840s to escape the devastating potato famine. It is also generally accepted that the Kid had a brother (or at least a half-brother) named Joseph, although it is unclear if he was older or younger than Henry. Surviving documents from these verifiable starting points reveal several enticing possibilities buried in the records.

It remains a mystery if McCarty was Catherine's maiden or married name, or if she simply assumed a paramour's surname. Records indicate that a Patrick McCarty married a Catherine Devane in New York City on June 19,1851. A son, Patrick Henry, was born in Ward 1, in lower Manhattan, on September 17, 1859. The child was baptized at St. Peter's Church on Barclay Street on September 28. Although it would be presumptuous to assume that this Patrick Henry is our Billy the Kid, considering the tens of thousands of Irish immigrants living in Ward 1 in 1859, the timeline is nevertheless correct, and, consequently, it remains a feasible theory.

The 1860 Federal census also has living in Ward 1 Catherine McCarty, age 29, along with Patrick McCarty, age 30, Bridget McCarty, age 7, and Henry McCarty, age 1. There are problems, however, in leaping to the conclusion that this Henry McCarty is our notorious outlaw. One problem is there is no record of Billy the Kid having a sister named Bridget. Another problem is that the 1860 census does not reflect the Kid's brother, Joseph, who is believed to have been born in 1854. Historians, however, have pointed out that there are inconsistencies in Joseph's pedigree, and that Joseph actually could have been the younger brother. Although Joseph's 1930 death certificate listed his age at 76 (which would make his birth year 1854), other records, such as a voter registration form from 1916, listed his birth year as 1863, making him the younger brother and therefore explaining the absence of Joseph on the 1860 census. Bearing in mind the substandard record-keeping in 1860, it is a viable possibility that the 1860 census from the First Ward of New York City does indeed include Billy the Kid.

New York City records also indicate that on November 20, 1859, an unnamed male child was born at 70 Allen Street, which borders the Five Points neighborhood, to the unmarried couple of Edward and Catherine McCarty. Although the 1860 census does not reflect this household, the 70 Allen Street address on the Lower East Side is routinely cited as the birthplace of the notorious Billy the Kid. The 1860 building no longer stands, having been razed in the 1930s when Allen Street was widened.

We do know that in 1867 Catherine, Henry, and his brother Joseph turned up in Indianapolis, Indiana, where Catherine met and ultimately married William Antrim. The Kid's stepfather would later state in a pension application that his wife's first husband "was named McCarty" and had "died in New York City."

In 1874 Catherine died in New Mexico, and the 13-year-old Henry started down the path to infamy and legend. Somewhere along the line, he picked up the alias "William Bonney," but he was universally known as "The Kid." The 1880 census for Fort Sumner, New Mexico lists a "Wm. Bonny" with a birthplace of Missouri. Since the Kid was clearly lying about his name, it is unlikely he would be truthful about his place of birth. In any event, he started his career committing petty crimes but graduated to homicide when, at age 17, he killed a teamster, who, in a classic case of underestimation, made a fatal mistake by bullying the Kid. In what would be a recurring theme for the Kid, he managed to escape from the Arizona jail that had tried to hold him and headed out to New Mexico.

Billy's timing was perfect. He arrived in the New Mexico territory just in time to become enmeshed in what would become known as the Lincoln County War. The "War" erupted in the late 1870s between rival cattle barons fighting over everything from the cost of goods to water rights to lucrative government contracts. For an entertaining crash course on the Lincoln County War, watch the 1970 Western film *Chisum*, starring John Wayne in the title role. Although historical inaccuracies abound, for the most part the names and the basic facts are correct. Young Billy was working for John Tunstall, a transplanted British rancher, who had taken a liking to the Kid and was aligned with Chisum against Lawrence Murphy and James Dolan. The murder of Tunstall in February 1878, allegedly on the orders of the Murphy faction, ignited unprecedented bloodshed between the two sides. By the time the fighting subsided five months later, over two dozen participants were dead, with the Kid doing

70 Allen Street , possible birth site of Henry McCarty- Billy the Kid.

more than his fair share. Billy emerged from the feud with Sheriff Pat Garrett on his trail, but the continuing exploits of the charismatic Billy the Kid were the fruitful subject of numerous newspaper exaggerations and dime novels.

Billy the Kid met his inevitable and violent end at the hands of his soon-to-be biographer, Sheriff Pat Garrett, on July 14, 1881, in Fort Sumner, New Mexico. Rumors almost immediately began to circulate that the Kid had not really been killed and that somebody else was buried in the grave whose marker bore his name. Periodically, through the decades, impostors would come forward claiming to be the Kid. Historians have almost unanimously agreed, however, that it is indeed Billy the Kid lying in the Fort Sumner grave.

While these historians can form a consensus as to the Kid's final resting place, they cannot reach the same certainty regarding the Kid's origin. But while it cannot be proved that he started his life on the streets of New York City, it also cannot be proved that he didn't. Even in the face of so much reasonable doubt, the circumstantial evidence points to Billy the Kid being a native New Yorker. Ironically, Billy's brother, Joseph, lived until 1930 and could have easily cleared up any inconsistencies about Billy's birth, had anyone thought to ask. Adding to historians' frustration over this untapped resource, Joseph, who was perceived as a local character in Denver, was interviewed by the *Denver Post* in 1928. In a monumental lapse of journalistic instinct, the reporter failed to make any inquiry whatsoever about Joseph's infamous sibling.

Cover of Pat Garrett's biography of Billy the Kid (Courtesy of Library of Congress LC-USZ62-87581).

EPILOGUE

As strange as it sounds, I wrote the introduction to the book just as I started to write it, and I'm writing the epilogue just as I am finishing up the text's first draft. As I got into the research, it became obvious that the subject matter was starting to include more of New York City's rich and diverse history than I had initially intended. It was simply too interesting to leave out.

As I stated in the introduction, I am not a historian. Although I did a fair amount of independent research and took advantage of the wonderful resources at the New York Historical Society and the Library of Congress, I think it is fair to concede that I have not uncovered any "new" information. What I hope I have done, in an entertaining manner, is cull information from myriad sources about the characters from the Old West that relate to New York City.

I have assumed that the reader has at least a passing interest in the Old West, as well as a familiarity with the personalities discussed in the book. But I hope you were nevertheless surprised by the extent to which New York City played host to the men and women of the Wild West.

Cube Structure,"Alamo," by Tony Rosenthal, located at Astor Place traffic island at Lafayette Street and East 8th Street.

NEW YORK'S ALAMO DEFENDERS

William Blazeby
Born in Norwich, England in 1795 but moved to New York. He went to the Alamo as part of the New Orleans Grays, a Texas volunteer regiment from Louisiana. At the time of the battle, he was a Captain, and commanded an infantry company.

Robert Cunningham
Born in Ontario County, New York in 1809 and served as an artilleryman in Captain Carey's company.

Lewis Dewall (or Duel)
Born in New York City in 1812. Records show that in 1832 he resided at 51 Lewis Street in lower Manhattan. At the time of the battle, he was a rifleman in Captain Robert White's infantry company.

Robert Evans
Born in Ireland in 1800 and immigrated to New York in 1827. He lived in New York City until relocating to Texas in 1836. At the time of the battle, he was a Major and the Chief of Ordinance at the Alamo. When it became obvious that all was lost, Evans unsuccessfully attempted to destroy the munitions stored in the Chapel with a lighted torch. Evan's heroic endeavor to try to prevent the munitions from falling into Mexican hands was, no doubt, the inspiration for Davy Crockett's death scene in 1960's *The Alamo*. In the film, John Wayne, as Crockett, fights his way to the entrance of the Chapel, and his dying act is tossing the torch into the munitions room blowing up the munitions (as well as himself).

Samuel B. Evans
Born in Jefferson County, New York in 1812.

John Hubbard Forsyth
Born in Avalon, New York in 1798. He was a Captain in the Texas volunteer cavalry unit. He was third in the Alamo chain of command after Travis and Bowie.

William D. Hersee
Born in England in 1805 but moved to New York. At the time of the battle, he served as an NCO in Captain Carey's artillery company.

Dr. William D. Howell
Born in Massachusetts in 1791 but practiced medicine in New York City. In addition to his medical duties, he served as a rifleman in Captain Blazeby's infantry company.

John Jones
Born in New York in 1810. He was a first ieutenant in Captain Blazeby's infantry company.

George C. Kimball (Kimble)
Born in New York in 1803 and a member of the Gonzales Ranging Company. Kimble County, Texas is named after him.

Dr. Amos Pollard
Born in Ashburnham, Massachusetts in 1803. He had a medical practice at 137 Delancy Street in New York City from 1828 to 1834. He was the principle surgeon at the Alamo.

John Tylee
Born in New York in 1795 and lived in New York City until relocating to Texas in 1834. He went to Texas armed with a Certificate of Good Character signed by the Mayor of New York City, C.W. Lawrence. At the time of the battle, he served as a rifleman.

BIBLIOGRAPHY

BOOKS

Anbinder, Tyler. *Five Points*. New York: Free Press, 2001

Cody, William F. *The Life of Buffalo Bill*. New York: Indian Head Books, 1991

Crockett, David, (ghost writer-William Clark). *An Account of Colonel Crockett's Tour to the North and Down East*. Philadelphia: Carey & Hart, 1835

Davis, William C. *Three Roads To The Alamo*. New York: HarperCollins, 1998

DeArment, Robert K. *Gunfighter in Gotham Bat Masterson's New York City Years*. Honolulu: Talei Publishers, 2005

Edmondson, J.R. *Alamo Story: From Early History to Current Conflicts*. Texas: Republic of Texas Press, 2000

Ellis, Edward Sylvester. *The Life of Colonel David Crockett: Comprising His Adventures*. Philadelphia: Power and Coates, 1884

Hatch, Thom. *The Last Outlaws*. New York: New American Library, 2013

Hauck, Richard Boyd. *Crockett A Bio-Bibliography.* Westport: Greenwood Press, 1982

Homberger, Eric. *The Historical Atlas of New York City.* New York: Holt Paperbacks, 1994 and 2005

Kennett, Lee. *Sherman: A Soldier's Life.* New York: HarperCollins, 2001

Lake, Stuart N. *Wyatt Earp, Frontier Marshal.* Boston: Houghton Mifflin, 1931

Leckie, Shirley A. *Elizabeth Bacon Custer and the Making of A Myth.* Norman: University of Oklahoma Press, 1993

Metz, Leon Claire. *The Shooters.* New York: Berkley Books, 1976

Morgan, Bill. *The Civil War Lover's Guide to New York City.* El Dorado Hills, Ca.: Savas Beatie LLC, 2013

Nolan, Frederick. *The Lincoln County War: A Documentary History.* New Mexico: Sunstone Press, 2009

O'Connell, Robert L. *Fierce Patriot: The Tangled Lives of William Tecumseh Sherman.* New York: Random House, 2014

Odell, George. *Annals of the New York Stage.* New York: Columbia University Press, 1937

Sagala, Sandra. *Buffalo Bill on Stage.* Albuquerque: University of New Mexico Press, 2008

Solmine, Lee. *The Life of John Martin (Giovanni Martin).* Boca-Raton: Universal-Publishers, 2012

Utley, Robert M. *Sitting Bull: The Life and Times of an American Patriot.* New York: Holt Paperbacks, 1993

Wallis, Michael. *David Crockett the Lion of the West.* New York: W.W Norton & Co., 2011

Wert, Jeffrey D. *Custer. The Controversial Life of George Armstrong Custer.* New York: Simon & Schuster, 1996

Wetmore Cody, Helen. *Last of the Great Scouts: The Life Story of Buffalo Bill Cody.* Iowa: Duluth Publishing Company, 1899

Wilson, Robert. *Mathew Brady Portraits of a Nation.* New York: Bloomsbury USA, 2013

Wolfe, Gerard R. *New York A Guide to the Metropolis.* New York: McGraw Hill, 1988

ARTICLES

Bridger, Bobby. "Sitting Bull and Buffalo Bill, The Shaman and the Showman." *Wild West*, December 2004

DeArment, R.K. "When The West Wasn't So Young, Fearless Bat Masterson Went To Live And Work In New York City." *Wild West*, June 2001

Batson, Jim. "Antique Bowies with a Touch of Mink." *Blade Magazine*, September 1996

Ernst, Donna B, "Butch, Sundance and Ethel Place Spent Time and Money in New York." *Wild West*, August 2010

Franz, Mary. "The Real Men of Deadwood." *Wild West*, August 2006

Gardner, Mark Lee. "The Life and Death of a Great Sheriff." *Wild West*, 2011

Hutton, Paul Andrew. "'It Was But A Small Affair' The Battle of The Alamo." Wild West, February 2004

Jay, Roger. "Bat Masterson Paladin of the Plains." *Wild West*, August 2009

Manz, William H. "Benjamin Cardozo Meets Gunslinger Bat Masterson." *New York State Bar Assoc. Journal*, July/August 2004

Patterson, Richard. "Wild Bunch Boss Butch Cassidy." *Wild West*, October 2002

Patterson, Richard. "Butch Cassidy's Surrender Offer." *Wild West*, February 2006

Robins, Anthony W. "The Hotel Albert, A History." New York: Thompson & Columbus Inc., 2011

Rosa, Joseph G., "Hickok's Last Gunfight." *Wild West*, December 2008

Salwen, Peter. "They Called Him The Belle Of New York." *New York Newsday*, November 29, 1985

Selcer, Richard and Donnell, Donna. "Last Word on the Famous Wild Bunch Photo." *Wild West*, December 2011

NEWSPAPERS

El Paso Times, Jul 19, 1902

Jamestown Weekly Alert, October 22, 1888

New York Evening Star, April 27, 28, May 1, May 2, May 23, 1834.

New York World, June 7, June 8, 1902.

New York Morning Telegraph, June 10, 1902

New York Times, December 11, 1872; April 1, 1873; July 15, 1886; October 12, 1894; April 3, 1901; June 7, June 8, June 9, June 10, 1902; April 2, 1905; May 15, 1910; April 5, 1933

New York Tribune, July 22, 1894

Salt Lake Herald, August 30, 1885

St. Paul Daily Globe, September 15, 1884

GOVERNMENT DOCUMENTS

U.S. Censuses

1870: San Francisco, Ca.; 1880 San Francisco, CA

1880: Fort Sumner, NM

1910: Los Angles, Ca., New York City, NY; 1920: New York City, NY.

New York City Directory
1922

WEB SITES

WWW.BUFFALOBILL.ORG
The Buffalo Bill Museum and Grave
WWW.DAYTONINMANHATTAN.BLOGSPOT.COM
Daytonian in Manhattan
WWW.NYSONGLINES.COM
Virtual walking tours of Manhattan
WWW.THEBOWERYBOYS.BLOGSPOT.COM
The Bowery Boys: New York City History

ARCHIVAL RESOURCES

Library of Congress, Washington, D.C.: Pinkerton criminal case files, Containers 87–89

INDEX

Merchants Exchange Building, 36
Metropole Hotel, 71–72, **72, 73**
Mexican-American War, 150
Mexico
  in battle at the Alamo, 40–42
  Texas as part of, 39
  See also Alamo
Missouri, 151, 156
Morning Telegraph (newspaper), 68, 75, 76
Mott, Valentine, 167–70, 168
Murphy, Lawrence, 181
My Darling Clementine (film), 144

A Narrative of the Life of David Crockett of the State of Tennessee (Crockett), 11
Native Americans
  In battles with Cody, 95
  at Cooper Union, **120,** 121
  Creek War against, 8
  Indian Removal Act on, 12
  at Little Bighorn, 94, 139–40
  Masterson on, 69
  portrayed in *The Scouts of the Prairie*, 82–83, 90
  Sherman and, 156–58
  Sitting Bull, 96–101, 97
  at Wounded Knee Massacre, 102
Newman, Paul, 49
New Mexico
  Billy the Kid in, 181
  Earp in, 145
  Garrett in, 173–75
  Native Americans in, 156
New York Aquarium, 35
New York City
as "Big Apple," 68
western figures in, 2
New York City Landmarks Commission, 169

New York Customs House, 36
New York Press Club, 133
New York Stock Exchange, 38
Niblo's Garden Theater, 82, 83
Niblo's Hotel, **84**

O.K. Corral (Tombstone, Arizona), 142, 144, 147
O'Kelley, Edward, 173
Oklahoma, Indian Territory in, 12
Omohundro, Jack, 82, **82**, 91
One Astor Plaza, 74
O'Neill, Eugene, 86
Outlaws of Missouri (play, Ford), 172

Park Avenue, **141**
Parker, Fess, 43
Parker, Robert LeRoy. *See* Cassidy, Butch
Park Place, **168**
Park Row, **29, 30**
Park Theatre, 28–31
Patton, Elizabeth (Crockett), 8
Peale, Charles Wilson, 18
Peale, Rubens, 18
Peale's Museum, 18–19, 19
Personal Memoirs of Ulysses S. Grant, 127
Pfaff's Beer Cellar, **126**, 126–27
photographers, 91–93
Pinkerton, Allan, 49
Pinkerton, Robert, 47
Pinkerton National Detective Agency, 49–50, 52–55, 57
  wanted poster by, **58**
Place, Etta, 47, 50–51, **53**, 55–59
  in Buenos Aires, 54
Place, Harry A. (Sundance Kid), 47, 55
Players Club, **131**, 132, 161
Poe, Edgar Allan, 28

Michael P. O'Connor